THE
AWFUL
TRUTH
ABOUT
PUBLISHING

THE AWFUL TRUTH ABOUT PUBLISHING

Why They Always Reject Your Manuscript...
And What You Can Do About It

JOHN BOSWELL

WARNER BOOKS

A Warner Communications Company

Warner Books, Inc., 666 Fifth Avenue, New York, NY 10103

W A Warner Communications Company

Printed in the United States of America
First Printing: September 1986
10 9 8 7 6 5 4 3 2 1

Designed by Giorgetta Bell McRee

Library of Congress Cataloging in Publication Data

Boswell, John, 1945–
    The awful truth about publishing.
        1. Publishers and publishing—United States.
2. Authors and publishers—United States.
3. Authorship.   I. Title.
Z471.B64 1986   070 5   86-40910
ISBN 0-446-51208-7

For Carol and Jonathan
———————— and ————————
the book publishing industry

ACKNOWLEDGMENTS

I would like to thank the many people throughout the publishing industry who have contributed their wisdom, expertise, and advice to this book. May all your titles become home videos.

I would also like to thank Betsy Ryan for her contribution to this book.

I owe particular debts of gratitude to Judy Linden, whose burst of enthusiasm got me going, to my editor Nansey Neiman, whose patience and understanding saw me through to the end, and to Margery Schwartz, Jackie Merri Meyer, Ann Schwartz, and my other friends at Warner Books who put up with a *lot,* and pretended not even to mind.

CONTENTS

THE
AWFUL
TRUTH
ABOUT
PUBLISHING

SECTION I

The Awful Truths

CHAPTER 1
Getting Down to Business

I t is not surprising that so many people dream of becoming published authors. It is, after all, such an attainable fantasy.

Walk into any bookstore, for instance, and you can't help but notice how many thousands of others have already managed to get themselves published. In fact, from a purely numerical standpoint, the odds are even better than you probably think: over *fifty thousand* new books were published just last year; nearly a *half million* during the last decade.

Yet as encouraging to aspiring authors as these numbers may at first seem they are actually quite deceptive. For the truth is that the vast majority of people who dream of getting published never even come close.

What most aspiring authors discover is that getting through to publishers—and getting any sort of considered response out of any of them—is about as easy as getting through to the Kremlin. It is almost as though a conspiracy were afoot to keep unpublished authors in a perpetual state of longing, and what becomes amazing is not how many new books get published each year, but how anyone ever manages to break into print.

If this has been your experience . . . if you have ever waited six agonizing months only to receive a form-typed rejection letter (addressed to "Sir or Madam") . . . if you half-suspect the box containing your manuscript was opened only for the purpose of inserting the rejection letter . . . if you are now convinced that the only way to turn a publisher's head is to change your name to Lee Iacocca or Jane Fonda . . . then please consider the following:

- Several years ago, an editor at Bantam Books received a publishing submission from a Mr. James Nourse. As part of his submission Mr. Nourse included a crude little self-published booklet, which, he maintained, held the solution to Rubik's Cube.

  The editor had recently received the Cube as a present from his son and, having already been confounded by it, was more than happy to give Mr. Nourse's work every consideration.

  Six months later, Mr. Nourse's original booklet, revised and expanded, was published under the Bantam imprint, and *The Simple Solution to Rubik's Cube* went on to sell over seven and a half million copies.

- Publishers don't expect to be accosted by a real estate salesman at a publishing convention, but that's exactly what happened one time to the chairman of Simon & Schuster. Bargain property in the Hamptons? No way. What the man wanted was S&S to publish his book on buying real estate with little or no money down. Several months and several drafts later, S&S did indeed publish Robert G. Allen's *Nothing Down*, marking the beginning of its three-year run on the bestseller list.

- Peter Workman, publisher of Workman Publishing's *Preppie Handbook*, remembers an unsolicited proposal he once received from a therapist which extolled the rather special virtues of hugging and kissing. Accompanying the proposal were several fanciful illustrations drawn by the therapist's girlfriend.

Not only did *Hugs and Kisses* go on to sell almost 300,000 copies, but its author and illustrator, Bruce Davis and Genny Wright, went on to become husband and wife (suggesting that fame and fortune are not necessarily publishing's only rewards).

- In the early 1970's, Doubleday received an unsolicited one-page letter addressed to "the Editor of *The Parallax View.*" Its sender, an unpublished novelist, wrote that he was a great admirer of that particular work and, since he had just completed a manuscript in a similar vein, suggested that the editor might respond favorably to his own work as well.

  The editor was sufficiently intrigued, but the novel that arrived was a disappointment. It was rejected, as were two others which followed in its wake.

  The aspiring novelist, now nearing despair, but now also in regular contact with the editor, mentioned he had one other manuscript, but it was not pure suspense as *The Parallax View* had been. It was more of a horror story.

  This time the editor liked what he saw, offered a modest $2,500 contract, and eighteen months later the publication of *Carrie* launched Stephen King's career.

These are only four of literally hundreds of similar (if not always as spectacular) success stories which are as much a part of book publishing as some of its more discouraging realities. Remember, no one is *born* published. Stephen King and every other author who has ever lived was, at one time, an outsider looking to get in.

These particular stories are recounted here, though, not simply to suggest that "this can happen to you too," but because they also illustrate something important about dealing with publishers, and that is that publishers are not nearly as unreachable (or insensitive) as they can often seem to be.

In fact, if you can get the *right idea in front of the right person at the right publishing house* (as the authors in all four of the above tales managed to do) you will find that most publishers, far from being unresponsive, will be pursuing you rather than the other way around.

Of course, selling your work to a publisher demands many of the same skills required to sell a product in any other business. And naturally, the more you know about your customer the better your chances of making a sale are going to be. So, before you can even begin to think seriously about what you should be submitting to publishers, you are first going to have to do some serious thinking about the publishing business itself.

This involves, first and foremost, understanding what you are truly up against and examining what may be some of your own preconceived notions about the publishing industry. Publishing, with its promise of overnight fame and fortune, may be one of the most idealized and misunderstood businesses in America. And many aspiring authors all but eliminate any real chance they have of getting published by dealing with the publishing industry as they would like it to be rather than as it actually is.

This, in fact, brings us to our first truth:

BOOK PUBLISHING IS A REAL BUSINESS

One of the biggest problems in dealing realistically with publishers is the romanticism that has grown up around the industry itself. And one of the great underlying romanticized notions is that somehow publishing is something more, or something less, than a real business—that the profit motive which is the driving force behind any other business or industry is somehow less important to publishers than discovering works of literary merit.

In truth, book publishing does like to think of itself as a little bit different from other businesses. And the people employed by publishing gravitate there because they are interested in the world of ideas and they do appreciate fine writing.

But what they soon discover is that publishers have to pay bills just like everyone else. And if they are to succeed and prosper, better first to find the next Robert Ludlum if they wish to take a chance later on the next Robert Lowell.

The bottom line to publishing is the bottom line. Random House must deal with the same economic factors as Dow Chemical, and the profit motive in publishing is just as strong (though the profit a bit harder to come by) as it is in any other business. And for aspiring authors, the best way to begin to understand the publishing business is to start thinking of it as acting, behaving, and operating like a *real* business.

This, for instance, might begin to suggest the wisdom in seeing your publishing submission less in terms of its literary merit and more in terms of its attractiveness as a business proposition. It may even suggest some of the factors that will go into a publisher's decision to "invest" in your book (some of which may not be unlike those that would occur to Dow Chemical in deciding to bring out a new floor wax!).

Most of all, however, it should begin to put a whole new perspective on some of the more conventional—and misleading—beliefs about how publishing operates.

One of the more commonly held images of publishing, for instance, is the one that has the editors sitting around the conference table discussing your manuscript as though it were a bottle of Chateau Lafite: "It's flawed of course, but it does have . . . elan."

In reality, unless you have been very calculating in your submission strategy, your manuscript never even got as far as an editor. Moreover, if all it has going for it is "elan," it's not going to get published anyway. And finally, while most publishing houses do hold weekly editorial meetings, the conversations there are much more likely to run to sales hooks and marketing handles than to effete editorial critiques.

Another common, totally wrong, perception is that of the easygoing, laid-back, semischolarly editor casually combing through the stacks of new submissions in search of something with which to while away the afternoon.

Again, in thinking of publishing as a "real business," would you have four hours in the middle of *your* business day to read a book? While publishing does remain a "gentleman's profession" compared to most businesses, it is hardly genteel. It is, in fact, such a hustling, bustling, competitive business that editors barely have time to read the manuscripts they have acquired, much less the unsolicited submissions to which they are already unfavorably predisposed.

What this means is that you can't sit back waiting to be discovered by some Maxwell-Perkins-in-the-making. You have to *make* it happen. You have to work aggressively, intelligently, and *cunningly* at getting your book noticed and making your submission stand out.

This, ultimately, is what this book is going to show you—what you need to know about the publishing business and, based on this knowledge, how to work intelligently at getting your book published.

It is going to show you how to come up with a salable idea, how to shape and focus that idea, and how to present it in its best possible light.

It is also going to show you how to get your idea in front of the right editor, how to grab that editor's attention, and how to keep him or her reading until your submission has "said" everything it needs to say.

But most importantly, it is going to show you the rules that govern the games publishers play, a strategy for getting around those rules, and the tactics that will get you out of the slush pile, onto an editor's desk, and in a form which can't be ignored, thrown away, or automatically rejected.

This is the endgame. Once you know how to make the right moves, editors will be left with no other choice than to give you at least as much care and consideration as they would authors with twenty books under their belt.

CHAPTER 2

Ten Awful Truths: How the Publishing Industry Works and Why It Often Doesn't

Several years ago a successful entrepreneur friend decided to take a shot at the book publishing business. "A book costs two dollars to produce," he said to me, "and sells for fifteen dollars, which means that somebody somewhere is making a big profit."

Today my friend owns a very successful business . . . which has nothing to do with books. After a two-year fling his parting comment was, "Only masochists should go into book publishing."

Why? If the economics that attracted my friend to it in the first place are true—and they are—why is it equally true that the vast majority of people in publishing can legitimately cry semipoverty?

That's because the business practices which dictate the very nature of the publishing business really are awful, making victims out of everyone involved in the publishing process, from the author, to the printer, to the publisher, to the bookstore owner.

Knowing what you're up against is the first step of any

successful strategic campaign. And so we are going to deal with ten of the publishing industry's more depressing and pervasive realities right now. It is these realities which conspire to make the publication of a book often seem less like the major event it should be, and more like a small, intimate—and thoroughly underpublicized—affair.

AWFUL TRUTH NUMBER ONE: THERE ARE 53,000 NEW TITLES PUBLISHED ANNUALLY

As encouraging as this number might be to aspiring authors (53,000 chances is more than you get at most things in life), it's also the awfulest of the awful truths. For, like snowflakes, no two books are exactly alike. While there are genre groupings, such as romances or self-help books, each new book is also unique and, ideally, should have its own unique promotion plan and marketing strategy. Maybe one out of every hundred new titles actually does.

To put this number—53,000—in perspective and to show how it wreaks havoc on the publishing business, compare it to the number of new products annually introduced in any other industry.

Suppose, for example, the automobile industry decided to introduce 53,000 new makes and models next year. What do you think that would do to their marketing strategies? And suppose that when half of them fail they decide: "What we need to do is bring out 53,000 more *new* makes and models next year." It's mind-boggling, but this is standard operating procedure in publishing.

If you think this analogy overstates the case, go into your local bookstore and look around. Now ask the book clerk if he has a particular title in stock, not by a bestselling author such as James Michener, but by a reasonably well known one.

Chances are very high that he won't have it in stock (but

will order it "if it's still in print"). Chances are almost as high that if he does have it in stock, he can't find it!

It would be very depressing for any author to realize that the person directly responsible for the sale of his or her book probably doesn't even know that it exists. But that is ultimately what happens when it is one of 53,000 new products dumped into the marketplace each year.

You might think that publishers would start to say, "We're publishing too many books." They do, but nothing is done about it. It's called The Right to Belly-up Through Free Enterprise.

Every publisher is afraid to publish fewer titles because they are afraid the results may be fewer sales. What they really want is all the *other guys* to publish fewer books.

AWFUL TRUTH NUMBER TWO:
YOU MUST SELL A BOOK THREE TIMES

Publishers sell books to bookstores on consignment, which creates that dreaded publishing word, *returns*. That means if a bookstore owner buys five copies of your book from the publisher, and sells only two of them, he can return the remaining three for full credit. If it's a paperback, he doesn't even have to return the whole book—just the *front cover*, or even just *part* of the front cover, which is unceremoniously ripped off and sent back in an envelope with a bunch of other covers.

This creates some interesting situations such as the following actual case history: A book is printed in Chicago and sent to the publisher's warehouse in New Jersey for distribution. It is then sent to a bookstore in Sacramento, but the bookstore is unable to sell it, so it is returned to the warehouse in New Jersey for full credit. Now it's ordered by a bookstore in Los Angeles, where it is duly sent, but the bookstore in L.A. can't sell it either. So once again it's returned to the warehouse in New Jersey for full credit.

That book, compliments of the U.S. Postal Service, has now crossed the country four and a half times but still remains unsold, stuck in a dingy warehouse, awaiting its next trip to who-knows-where, maybe Hawaii.

Returns might be manageable if it only affected one out of every ten or twenty books. But in the hardcover business, for every ten books shipped, *three are returned.* In the paperback business, for every ten books shipped, *five are returned.*

No one is really sure how this horrible practice got started but it probably goes back a hundred years or so to when publishing was a hobby for the sons of wealthy families. Since money was hardly a concern, the publisher/scion would say to the bookseller, "Here are some of my books. If you sell them, fine. If you don't, we'll give you your money back." Returns are now such an accepted practice that when the last book is sold in some future millennium, it will probably be sold returnable.

What this means is that you have to sell your manuscript or proposal three times, first to the publisher, who turns it into a book, second to a bookstore owner, who agrees to stock it, and finally to the customer who actually pays real money and carries it out the front door. Only then can a book be considered officially sold.

For the aspiring author this is, fortunately, not quite as alarming as it sounds. For if you can satisfy, first and foremost, the needs and interests of the actual consumer, the person who puts money down, the other two are likely to fall in line. If you can shape and focus an idea for a book that readers want to buy, then the publisher will probably want to buy it from you, and the bookseller will probably want to buy it from the publisher.

AWFUL TRUTH NUMBER THREE:
DISTRIBUTION AND FEEDBACK ARE
INEFFICIENT

Part of the problem is returns, but the other problem is time. Have you ever gone into a bookstore and asked the clerk to order a book for you? He never says, "It will be here on Tuesday." What he usually says is, "We'll call you in four to six weeks."

There are many reasons for this, but the main one is that when you're selling something for $15, it's not very profitable to send it by Federal Express.

The bookstores don't help the situation. If five people come in the same day and ask for the same book, does the bookstore order ten copies? To be on the safe side they may order six.

Moreover, when you have several hundred products in one store, all of which look about the same except for their covers, it can get very confusing. Several years ago, Erica Jong's steamy novel *Fear of Flying* was found in the "Travel" sections of several bookstores and in some others under "Aviation" and "Psychology."

AWFUL TRUTH NUMBER FOUR:
BOOK PUBLISHING HAS NO TEST
MARKETING APPARATUS

Your chances of getting published would be greatly enhanced if a publisher could offer the following response:

> Thank you for your recent manuscript on growing
> avocados. We are intrigued by the concept, but
> are unsure of its wide market appeal. We would
> like to offer an option payment of $500 and test

> it in selected bookstores around the country. If your
> book performs well we will offer a full publishing
> contract.

This will never happen. The market test, a fundamental first stage in virtually all consumer product business, doesn't exist in book publishing. There are two reasons for this. First, the start-up costs or fixed costs, meaning the costs of setting the book in type, printing and binding it, are too expensive to justify a test printing of several hundred copies. Second, it's those damn 53,000 new titles again. Who has the time?

A publisher once remarked to me, "You test-market a book by publishing it." This is the ultimate publishing irony. Even when a book does surprise a publisher and performs beyond expectations, it's often too late. The publisher is already concentrating on his new list of titles and the successful "test market" is old news. In other words: "We can't worry about one successful book. We've got 53,000 new ones to get out!"

AWFUL TRUTH NUMBER FIVE: BOOKS ARE NOT FOOD, SHELTER, OR CLOTHING

Books sustain the mind, not the body, and are therefore not considered to be one of life's essentials. Sadly, books aren't even a popular form of entertainment. Most Americans read a book only when there is nothing on the tube and no other diversions available to them.

Ten years ago a blockbuster bestseller like *The Godfather* or *The Exorcist* sold twelve million copies. Today a huge bestseller sells three million copies—or to about *one percent* of the population. This is probably the most depressing of the Awful Truths for people within the publishing industry. Sometimes people who work in publishing feel like all the

A BOOK'S TIME LINE

Most books are signed up from a proposal, and the author is given anywhere from six to twelve months to deliver the completed manuscript. The editorial give-and-take that follows ordinarily consumes another two or three months, though depending on the amount of editorial work required this process can take up to a year or even longer.

Once a manuscript has been edited and accepted by the house, it will be scheduled for publication, usually not less than six to eight months later. During this period the manuscript will be copy-edited, designed, set in type in the form of "galleys" or "page proofs" (which are returned to the author for one final perusal), and forwarded to the printer approximately six to eight weeks before publication date.

Books are actually printed and bound in a matter of two or three days. The soup-to-nuts process, however, from the signing of a contract to actual publication, averages fifteen months to two years.

people who actually buy and read books could fit at one time into the Astrodome.

What this means to you, the author-in-waiting, is that reading, facing competition from VCR's, movies, TV, and video games, is always in danger of becoming the Incredible Shrinking Pastime. What this also means is that there aren't nearly as many people out there anxious to read your book as you might think there are.

As industries go, publishing is tiny. The hard numbers are that publishing is a $10-billion-a-year industry. That's everything—science books, textbooks, encyclopedias, novels, book club editions, dictionaries, Bibles—anything that has a cover and printed pages. That means that there are over fifty American companies that are larger than the entire publishing industry.

Moreover, the part of the industry that interests you—trade book publishing (novels and general non-fiction sold through bookstores)—is only a $4-billion-dollar-a-year industry.

With 53,000 new titles coming out each year, or about 500,000 new titles in the past decade, even with an elementary understanding of mathematics, you can begin to see why almost no one makes money in book publishing. When you take all of these books and divide them among the people who actually buy books, the average hardcover book ends up selling about 5,000 copies.

AWFUL TRUTH NUMBER SIX: A MASSIVE PROMOTION BUDGET WON'T BUY THIRTY SECONDS ON "SIXTY MINUTES"

The big guys, the Micheners, the Ludlums, American Presidents, and Hollywood stars, may get up-front advertising commitments of $100,000 to $150,000. What do you figure your book is going to get?

Don't ponder the answer too long because even the vast majority of published writers whose books didn't make it to the bestseller list are convinced in the back of their minds that their publishers sabotaged them by failing to promote their books. The awful truth is that almost *no* book is given the advertising it deserves. (Every year, the automobile industry spends more money on promotion than the entire publishing industry makes in profit.)

But take heart, the good news/bad news is that even if a publisher agreed to spend a million dollars promoting your book it probably wouldn't matter. You can't make a book sell simply by throwing money at it.

The myth prevails, even among experienced authors, that

a book can be promoted by advertising. However, several times in recent years, wealthy individuals have agreed to help finance the publication of their books with their own money, usually kicking in an excess of a million dollars to the publisher's ad campaign. Most of these books have not sold especially well, or any more than they probably would have anyway.

The truth of the matter is that with the exception of brand name authors like Sidney Sheldon or Mario Puzo (where advertising lets their readers know they have a new book out), most books are sold by word of mouth, not through ads in *The New York Times Book Review.*

Just take a look at the way you buy books; it's often on a friend's recommendation. This is why it is so important that your book idea appeal, first and foremost, to the reader—the book buyer. For without the word-of-mouth network, no amount of promotion dollars is going to make your book sell.

AWFUL TRUTH NUMBER SEVEN: BLINK AND YOU MAY MISS YOUR BOOK'S PUBLICATION

The copyright term of a book is life of the author plus fifty years, and while the copyright laws are there for your protection, the unfortunate truth is that they protect you for a lot longer than you probably need to be. It is the exceptional hardcover book that remains in print for more than a year, and even most of these hardy survivors are gone within three years. (And these are just industry averages: there are many books that go out of print in six months.)

The paperbacks (known as mass market paperbacks or rack-sized paperbacks) that you see in drugstores, grocery stores, airports, and newsstands won't even be around that long. They are distributed by magazine wholesalers, and are treated in much the same manner as last month's issue of

Playboy. If it's still around four weeks later, it's time to take it off the stands, rip off the cover, and return it to the publisher.

It's sad but true that a jar of mayonnaise will most likely have more staying power than your book.

AWFUL TRUTH NUMBER EIGHT: EVERY BOOK IS UNIQUE, BUT ALMOST NONE CAN BE TREATED AS SUCH

The Joy of Sex is about as different from *The Joy of Cooking* as a Mack truck is from a Toyota. Publishers, however, have been forced by the sheer number of titles they process to establish systems where most books are promoted, displayed, and treated much the same. As a result, books that might have tremendous appeal in a special market—a gourmet cookbook in gourmet stores, for instance—will most likely never end up there. Or a book that is precisely what the reader is looking for will be one of several hundred on the same general topic, and when the reader does happen upon that specific book, it is almost always by chance.

A bookstore is like a supermarket that contains nothing but generic canned goods: all about the same size and shape; all packaged similarly; no special promotion or distinctive features to speak of; and with the only real clue of contents being the words on the "label." Perhaps no other type of consumer has to work harder at simply finding out what he or she wants to buy than a reader looking for a book.

This "generic problem," of course, is no more than a reiteration of the aforementioned snowflake factor, a symptom of the too-many-books disease rather than a cause. But it is being treated separately here to emphasize something important about how books are purchased and the writer's role in helping to create buyer demand.

Book buyers tend to be *browsers,* in part because it's fun (a reader in a bookstore is like a kid in a candy shop), in part out of necessity (the buyers are preconditioned to looking around for what they want), and in part because it is all but impossible not to be (they must pass several thousand books on their way to purchasing the new Michener). As a result, the impulse buy accounts for more than half of all bookstore sales.

Since publishers can't be much help, it is therefore primarily the writer's responsibility to shape and focus his or her concept to stand out in a faceless crowd and to catch the browser's eye ("Now *that's* a book I'd like to read").

There will be a great deal later on about targeting your book to its audience, and this is the reason behind it: in a world where everything looks, and is treated, pretty much the same, it is being different, special or unique—setting yourself apart—that usually wins the day.

AWFUL TRUTH NUMBER NINE: BAD AIR DRIVES OUT THE GOOD

Publishers are in such an ongoing competitive battle they invariably manage to kill the goose that lays the golden egg. A trend or topic gets hot; all the publishers jump in, many of them with bad quickie books; the trend is saturated; then a year later, the trend is dead altogether. The plethora of titles in a particular category can strangle it. That's what happened to gothics and is in the process of happening to romances. The excess of titles turns them into lame genres and kills off all but the hardiest of survivors.

This bandwagon approach to publishing means that if something's hot, everyone jumps aboard. The result is that although you may have a good idea, by the time your proposal lands on a publisher's desk, it's the ninety-seventh one of its kind he's seen that week.

AWFUL TRUTH NUMBER TEN:
THE BAD GETS WORSE

Several years ago, the dynamic young editorial director of a major publishing house abruptly resigned, catching the rest of the industry by surprise. Months later we had lunch and I asked him why, after such a meteoric rise through the ranks, he had suddenly decided to step down.

"The whole publishing process began to seem like a losing proposition to me," he said. "I found we were buying a lot of marginal books just to keep the presses rolling and that kept us from giving enough attention to the more deserving books. It was like this giant mouth that constantly had to be fed. And the more we fed it the hungrier it got."

Faced with the returns problem, a mystifying distribution system, and more books than anyone could possibly cope with, publishers must run faster and faster just to stay in place.

Each book is unique, special—and fragile—in its own way. But, again like snowflakes, too many of them become an avalanche and crush the systems built to contain them. Soon, practically every book seems to fall through, if not one crack, then the next one.

Consider the following:

- The titillating confessions of *The Happy Hooker* are mistakenly bound into the middle of the inspirational paperback *Brian's Song*.
- A well-known author (whose most famous work was, at the time, riding atop every bestseller list) threatens to sue his publisher. Just as his book is cresting in popularity, his publisher, it seems, has run out of stock.
- An author makes a full day of publicity appearances in Minneapolis, but there's not a single copy of his book in all of Minnesota.

- An author's book is published, with her name misspelled on the cover.
- The biography of a baseball superstar is acquired by an enthusiastic sports editor. Three weeks later the editor leaves for another house, and the book is reassigned to an enthusiastic cookbook editor.
- A novelist delivers the final section of a book it has taken her two years to write. "We love Part IV," her editor says, "but we can't seem to locate Parts I through III. I hope you kept a copy..."
- An author comes across his book in the store two months before its pub date. When he calls his editor demanding to know why he wasn't informed of his own book's publication, his editor replies, "Don't blame me. No one told me either."

Out of stock, out of time, or out of luck, these are all examples of the kinds of garden-variety blunders that happen in publishing every day—the inevitable result of overloaded systems and overextended people.

To add to the chaos, by the time a book is published it is often old news. Editors must necessarily spend the majority of their time acquiring new books and editing manuscripts. When one of their babies is published six to ten months after the editing process has ended, it may very well be an orphan, its editor and chief benefactor having been forced to abandon it for the more pressing chores of acquiring and editing. A system that begs for an answer to the question "Who's in charge here?" evolves into a matter of "No one's in charge here" by the time the book actually comes out.

Publishers and editors are as much the victims of this system as their authors are. They would all like to do something about it, but everyone is already spread so thin, no one ever gets around to addressing the larger problems that cause all the little ones. So the problems snowball and self-perpetuate.

AND NOW THE GOOD NEWS:
THE MAGIC FACTOR

In spite of these awful truths, there is one phenomenon about book publishing that is almost magical in the way it works: a book can survive no matter how much a publisher benignly ignores it or unintentionally tries to kill it. If a book strikes a responsive chord (not necessarily an important book or a literary masterpiece but one that connects with or meets the needs of a sizable audience), it will not only survive but thrive.

Amazingly and inexplicably many books that were given absolutely no chance by their publishers have gone on to become enormously successful bestsellers.

In Search of Excellence, for instance, which sold 1.5 million copies in hardcover and even more in paperback, was initially published with a first printing of under 10,000 copies (less than one copy per bookstore!).

Going back a few years, two books published within months of each other, *I'm O.K., You're O.K.* and *Jonathan Livingston Seagull*, were both launched with printings of less than 5,000 copies. Since both were short books by unknown authors, even those few stores that did order them displayed them spine-out (i.e. as on a library shelf). How those first books were ever found by their readers still remains a mystery.

Both, of course, not only went on to become multimillion-copy sellers, but were the first two books to break the million-dollar barrier for paperback rights.

In fairness to their publishers, all three of these titles caught a market at its cusp. Yet there are many, many other titles which have had similar, if not quite as spectacular, publishing histories.

So don't give up yet, for the simple wonderful truth is that you have the magic factor going for you. In spite of all the awful truths that conspire to kill it, if your book has innate appeal, then it will also have staying power, and it is already on its way to becoming publisher-proof.

CHAPTER 3
Know Your Enemy: The Anatomy of a Publishing House

The public's ideas about a publishing house are tainted by myth and misconceptions. (Even the fact that publishing companies are often referred to as "houses" is misleading, conjuring up, as it does, the image of cozy cottages filled with parlors, libraries, and reading rooms.) To enter a publishing house is thought to be entering a glamorous universe of intellectual repartee and literary musings, a world in which editors smoke pipes, spend hours discussing the Great American Novel, and comb the new submissions looking for a bright young talent who can be nurtured into the next Hemingway.

In reality, I can think of only one editor who smokes a pipe (indeed, the majority of editors are women), and the glamour can be summed up in a comment I once heard from an editor who was so mired in manuscripts she hadn't seen the light of day for months. "Life," she sighed, "is lonely at the middle."

Though publishing is rarely as glamorous as it is thought to be—all publication parties and authors' luncheons—it can be fun, energizing, and stimulating. If it weren't for all those books...

The most unglamorous part of publishing is the workload,

those 53,000 books again. Most editors are overworked and underpaid and spend the majority of their days "moving the merchandise." This includes attending scheduling meetings; holding cover conferences; writing jacket blurbs; attending sales conferences; composing catalogue copy and sales information sheets; putting out fires; and returning all the phone calls that these activities entail. Editing is done sporadically; reading is done in bed at midnight; and thinking is confined to next morning's shower.

It may already be occurring to you that the easier you make an editor's job, the better your chances are going to be of getting a considered response. But before getting more specific about how editors spend their days and how some knowledge of the workings of a publishing house will work to your benefit, it is helpful first to have a working knowledge of some of the most common publishing terms.

JARGON

Like any other business, publishing has its own jargon. The following list is limited to those publishing terms that are most relevant to the aspiring author.

Trade Book. "Trade" in most industries means "of or to the trade." In publishing, "trade" (also called general books) means just the opposite—books sold to the general public, primarily through bookstores. This includes everything from novels to how-to books to biographies, just about everything, in fact, *except* textbooks, technical and scientific books, mail order books, and certain professional books such as medical and legal reference works. Unless you're a nuclear physicist writing for other nuclear physicists, your book, in all probability, is a *trade book*.

Slush. As in "slush pile." Also called "unsols" (short for unsolicited) and "over-the-transoms," a term referring to the open windows over doors in old office buildings (legend has it that aspiring authors would pitch their manuscripts "over the transom" into the publisher's office). If you address your submission to the "Editorial Department" or "The Editors" this is where your submission is likely to land—and stay until it is returned to you with a form rejection letter.

Copy-Edit. This is what people often think an editor does when an editor edits. It isn't. Copy-editing is the process of checking facts for accuracy and correcting such things as spelling, punctuation, and grammar. This is a totally separate function performed by a totally separate department, aptly named the copy-editing department. An editor working in the editorial department is more concerned with such things as a manuscript's pacing, structure, and clarity of thought. This doesn't mean that it's okay to submit a filthy, marked-up proposal filled with misspellings and poor grammar. It does mean that a misspelled word is not grounds for automatic rejection.

Seasons. Although books are published year-round, they are generally grouped into two seasons, spring and fall. This is the result of most publishing companies kicking off each new list with semiannual sales conferences, usually held in June for the fall list and in December for the spring list. The paperback houses are an exception; they issue twelve monthly lists. There is, however, no best time or worst time to submit a proposal or manuscript. Publishers are open to the right submission any time of the year.

List. This is, literally, a list of the publisher's books. Books just published or about to be published are called the "front list"; books already published are called the "back list." "List" also refers to the spring and fall lists.

Imprint. A specific line of books within a publishing house usually defined by its own name and colophon. Perennial

Library, for instance, is one of Harper & Row's trade paper-back imprints.

Line. Publishers often refer to an imprint within their house as a "line."

Line Editor. To "line edit" a manuscript means to tighten sentences, smooth over transitions, etc., as opposed to a major overhaul. If your manuscript is only in need of line editing it means it is in pretty good shape.

Reprints. This is the term that has to do with "waiting until it comes out in paperback." The reprint rights of the more popular hardcovers are sold to the paperback houses.

Originals. This is a paperback term. Ten years ago the vast majority of paperbacks were hardcover reprints. Now over half are "originals," or manuscripts purchased and "originated" by the paperback house.

Categories. There will always be a market for certain fictional genres and these genres are called categories. Examples of categories are romances, westerns, sports books, mysteries, science fiction, and humor. With rare bestselling exceptions (such as *Dune* in science fiction or any western by Louis L'Amour) these books sell predictably and well enough to keep doing them. Most category fiction is published as original paperbacks.

Title. This is a frequently used synonym for book. When a publisher says, "We have thirty-five titles on our spring list," he's referring to books.

Remainders. Though this isn't really a publishing term you need to know, it is included here to help explain why publishers will not be interested in publishing your collection of color photographs of our National Parks.

Remainders are books which are sold in bookstores and by direct mail for a fraction of their cover price. A book is "remaindered" either because the publisher has over-printed or has been inundated by returns and is selling off stock at a fraction of its cost.

Another type of remainder is the "discount book." These are books that are printed expressly for the purpose—i.e. they appear to be $19.95 books that have been marked down, but in fact they were always intended to be sold at a fraction of that price. These books are often created by book producers or "packagers" around extant color plates. A book entitled *The Wonderful World of Flowers*, for example, might be produced around stock color photos from a seed company.

The presence of these colorful, glossy books in stores fosters the common misassumption that they represent an attractive opportunity for aspiring writers. They don't. Only a handful of publishers will even consider books that require the expensive process of color reproduction. In fact, as a general rule, the more photos and illustrations your book demands, the less salable it is going to be to a publisher.

HOW A PUBLISHING COMPANY WORKS

A publishing company is structured like the two hemispheres of the brain: the spatial, creative half, or the editorial department; and the logical, pragmatic half, or the sales (or marketing) department. An editor will ask, "Should this book be published?" for which there are a number of reasons to say yes (commercial; importance; a steady seller; keep the author happy). A sales director will ask one question: "How many can I get into the bookstores?" The editors usually have a numerical advantage because they are all located in-house, while most of the sales department is on the road. But if a sales director vehemently opposes a title he can usually nix it, or at the very least lower its print order.

When the two sides can't agree on the potential of a book,

that's when the publisher, to whom both departments report, gets to do his job.

THE EDITORIAL DEPARTMENT

The editorial department is usually under the auspices of one person, called either the editorial director or the editor-in-chief, with the second-in-command usually referred to as the executive editor. The number of senior editors within a house, anywhere from one to fifteen, is, obviously, determined by the size of the house or imprint and the nature of the list. In addition to senior editors there can be any number of associate editors and editorial assistants, the latter being a title that allows publishers to pay less for secretarial duties than they would have to otherwise.

While almost every book is sponsored by an individual editor a new acquisition is rarely made unilaterally. Acquisitions usually require the consent of the editorial director, the passive acquiescense of other editors, and the encouragement of other divisions within the house, particularly the marketing and subsidiary rights departments. Based on seniority and past performance, some editors do have the right to make any acquisition they want up to a certain price. However, this right is rarely exercised without at least some enthusiasm from others, inasmuch as these others will be called upon later to help make the book a success.

Though the publisher—meaning the person with that title—is charged with balancing bottom-line realities with editorial enthusiasms, the best publishers almost always possess a strong editorial sense and a decidedly editorial bent. The publisher is almost always consulted on any major acquisition, and occasionally will act as the behind-the-scenes head of the editorial department.

In addition to acquiring and editing manuscripts, the editorial department is also the center of activity within the publishing house and is responsible for the overall coordination of the many stages and functions of getting a book published. (Curiously, where the managing editor is often the top editorial title at magazines and newspapers, in book publishing it refers to the editor in charge of trafficking and coordination.)

Though most editors will lean slightly toward either fiction or non-fiction they are all expected to be generalists and to possess a broad awareness of the world around them. In other words, even if an editor has never acquired or edited a cookbook before he or she is presumed to know a good one when it comes in and is charged with making sure that it gets into the hands of the right editor within the house.

THE MARKETING DEPARTMENT

Until several years ago there was no such thing as a marketing director in publishing, though many sales directors, in need of a promotion, were given that title. But publishers have been forced to become more sophisticated, and these days, more often than not, the sales department is one facet of a more diversified marketing department, which also explores new and different approaches to selling books, coordinates publicity and promotion activities, and figures out new ways to get a book into the hands (and into the minds) of its public.

A very savvy marketing director of a major publishing house once told me, "Marketing begins before you acquire the book. In fact, the single major marketing decision is the decision to acquire it." Another put it a different way: "When we acquire a book we don't need to know the exact profile of its reader or what the cover blurb should be. But the '-able' words should already be occurring to us: Is this marketable? Promotable? Salable? Is this publishable?"

In the best-run publishing houses the editorial department and the marketing department "talk the same talk." The editors will appreciate and understand publishing's marketing realities and factor them into their acquisition decisions, and the marketing people will demonstrate editorial sensitivity and often make valuable editorial recommendations. In the poorly run publishing houses the marketing and editorial departments often seem to exist on different planets.

THE OTHER DEPARTMENTS

In addition to the editorial and marketing departments, there are five additional primary departments and a number of support departments that round out the typical publishing house.

The Primary Departments:

The Art Department. Designs covers and dust jackets and commissions cover art. Usually requires the sign-off of the publisher, the editor, and the sales department. *Important Note:* Publishers consider the covers of their books a private domain. Unless you are Norman Mailer, a publisher is not interested in seeing your cover sketch as part of your submission.

The Production and Design Department. Designs the inside of a book, works with the printer, and turns a manuscript into something you can actually buy in a bookstore.

The Promotion Department. Creates and places ads; creates point-of-sale and other display materials for the bookstores.

The Publicity Department. Gets copies of the book to reviewers, arranges media coverage, and schedules authors' media tours.

Warehouse and Distribution. Receives the printed, jacketed books from the printer and gets them to the bookstores.

SUBSIDIARY RIGHTS

When a book is published, the act of publication creates a certain body of "rights" to the book in addition to the publisher's right to print and publish it. The responsibility of the "Sub Rights Department" is to exploit as many of these rights as possible on behalf of both the publisher and author. The following table lists the usual "splits" of income from the sales of these rights.

- Paperback rights: 50% to the author; 50% to the publisher
- Book club rights: 50% to the author; 50% to the publisher
- Translation into foreign language rights: 75% to the author; 25% to the publisher
- British rights: 80% to the author; 20% to the publisher
- Serialization rights:
  first serial (excerpts sold to a magazine that appear before your book's publication): 90% to the author; 10% to the publisher
  Second serial (excerpts sold to a magazine that appear after your book's publication): 50% to the author; 50% to the publisher
- Performance rights: These include movie and TV rights. These rights are almost always retained by the author.

The Support Departments:

The support departments include copy-editing, subsidiary rights (sale of book rights to clubs and magazines), special sales (for instance, getting a natural foods cookbook into natural food stores), and the contracts, bookkeeping, and royalty departments.

THE EDITOR

It has been said that editing is more a passion than a profession, which is one way of trying to explain why anyone would take on such a thankless job of such unrelenting demands.

In addition to reading and editing, which are usually done at home after work and on weekends, editors must commit themselves to an interminable amount of busywork just to keep the whole process moving.

Their days are usually filled with the nuts and bolts of the job—attending editorial and sales meetings and writing catalogue and jacket copy—and an ongoing hustle for new acquisitions—chasing after hot books, commissioning others, and responding to submissions from agents. Since major books are often multiply submitted (sent to several houses simultaneously) it is not unusual for an editor to spend several days getting his or her facts and figures together only to lose the book to another house.

Moreover, editors are the publisher's front men—their eyes and ears are their first line of defense. They must keep up with what's going on out there in the real world, and in the rest of publishing. And if a question needs to be answered or a problem solved, either inside or outside the house, it is almost always the editor who gets the first phone call.

Finally, authors, simply by the nature of their work, are not the least demanding group of people in the world. When authors can't write they want to talk and guess who they call? Editors will often serve several roles to their writers, including therapist and confessor. Huge chunks of time and energy are also spent placating some authors, cajoling others, and, around deadline time, chasing after those who have gone into hiding.

All this might be manageable if an editor could only work on several books or one list at a time. Instead, editors are constantly bouncing from the books they are acquiring to the books they are editing, to the books they are about to publish, to the books they have already published. Schedule juggling alone becomes a fulltime job. Ten, even twenty books at a time might be fine, but a couple of hundred titles built up over several years is more than any sane person should be asked to cope with. The bottom line to all this activity is that when editors meet themselves coming and going they don't even have time to wave hello.

For the aspiring writer, this may have already begun to suggest an unfortunate publishing paradox. As an unpublished author, *you don't fit into an editor's workday.* Thus, the paradox: in order to get published you must deal with an editor, but an editor's job—what he or she gets paid for—does not include dealing with you.

That's right. If you've ever submitted anything to a publisher, your suspicions can now be confirmed. An editor probably never even saw your work much less took the time to read it. An editorial assistant six months out of college *was* probably the one sitting in sole judgment of your masterpiece—if you were lucky. It is almost as likely that it was the receptionist or an off-duty phone operator, or even an office temp—i.e. whoever was assigned the task of going through the slush pile and inserting form rejection letters—who was the ultimate and only arbiter of your work.

It should be pointed out that contrary to popular opinion publishers do not delight in this callous treatment of unpublished authors. It is simply a business judgment they are all forced to make. The odds of finding something publishable in the slush pile are infinitesimally small, and if the needle is thrown out every once in a while along with the rest of the haystack, then so be it. It may not be fair to the needle owner, but it is a cost of doing business that every publisher readily accepts.

Is there any way to beat the system and skip the slush pile altogether? In fact, the system for efficiently dismissing unsolicited submissions is so rigid that getting around it is a fairly simple procedure, which will be discussed in detail later on.

For the moment, however, the most important thing for you to appreciate about a publishing house is the *workload* and the toll it takes on the editors. For even if you do manage to skip the slush pile, an otherwise sympathetic editor is likely to make unsympathetic judgments about your work based on nothing more than the overwhelming press of other business.

Understanding these pressures and how to excerbate them, begins with your ability to get inside the editor's head, to put yourself in the editor's shoes and to appreciate from that point of view the demands that are already being made on his or her time.

It is from this perspective that you will best be able to deal with the many obstacles that you and your submission are going to face.

A FEW WORDS ABOUT FORMAT or WHY YOU CAN'T TELL THE EDITOR WITHOUT A TAPE MEASURE

One final point needs to be made about the inner workings of a publishing house and that is that the size and shape of a book (and the thickness of its cover) can actually determine who will be handling it internally.

Today, most publishing houses consist of several different imprints under one publishing roof, all sharing common services such as sales and warehousing but each with its own editor or editorial department. Since imprints are often created to identify certain formats, in order to figure out to whom you should be submitting your work some knowledge of publishing's three basic formats is practically essential:

Hardcovers. The stiff inflexible cover is a dead giveaway. Hardcover books invariably have "hard" covers and retail for anywhere from $9.95 up to $75, for full-color art books. Standard hardcover size is 6″ × 9″.

Mass Market Paperbacks. Also called "rack-sized paperbacks" and "pocket books" (though Pocket Books is actually the corporate name of one of the major paperback companies).

Mass market paperbacks are all about the same size (4³⁄₁₆″ × 6¾″) so they can fit in the racks that you find in drugstores, K-Marts and supermarkets. The majority of mass market paperbacks—approximately 60 percent of them—are sold outside of bookstores and are distributed by jobbers and wholesalers, who may also be distributing magazines and newspapers, or even products other than books. This wide, scattershot distribution is why the returns are so heavy in the mass market business and the distribution is so unwieldy. While there is a finite number of bookstores in the United States, the number of paperback outlets is practically infinite.

There are eight major mass market paperback houses, which comprise 80 to 90 percent of the mass market paperback business. They are: Bantam; Warner; Pocket Books; New American Library (Signet); Berkley/Jove; Ballantine/Fawcett/Del Rey; Avon; and Dell. *

Mass market houses reprint all the major hardcover fiction and publish most of the category fiction. As a result, approximately four out of every five mass market paperback titles are fiction.

Trade Paperbacks. This is the most freewheeling format. Most trade paperbacks are published in two standard sizes, 6″ × 9″ and "large format" 8½″ × 11″, though practically any book published today that is neither a hardcover nor a mass market is considered a trade paperback.

---

*Most mass market houses now have their own hardcover and trade paperback lists, but the mentality is still mass market; i.e. they take a bolder, more aggressive position with their hardcovers than a traditional hardcover publisher might. In "looking for the big numbers," however, they are also much more selective, and publish maybe only ten to twenty hardcovers a year.

Unlike most paperbacks, trade paperbacks are distributed primarily through bookstores. The trade paperback format is often used to keep quality fiction and certain classic books in print and as the backlist form for many previous non-fiction bestsellers.

Format is also a numbers game, the theory being the cheaper a book is to produce, the lower the retail price and therefore the more one can sell. A hardcover, for instance, that retails for $15.95 would retail at $7.95 in trade paperback, and $3.95 in mass market. While an average first printing of a hardcover book is 10,000 copies, the average for a trade paperback is 25,000 copies and for a mass market, 100,000 copies. As these numbers may indicate, the relative popularity and appeal of a subject often influences the format in which publishers choose to publish it.

It's a little bit like the chicken or the egg riddle, but if you can begin to envision the most appropriate format for your book based on your subject matter, this will be one of your best submission clues later on. For instance, you may have just completed the best biography of Marcel Proust ever written. But you're not going to sell it to a mass market house because Proust is not a subject of great popular interest. Or you may have just written a book called *The World's Best Dirty Jokes.* Your odds of getting it published are best at a mass market paperback house.

In using format as a submission clue, don't kid yourself. There aren't, for instance, ten million people out there dying to read about Marcel Proust. On the other hand, your best bet for selling category fiction is the mass market houses.

It is also helpful to ask yourself, "What does my book 'look' like?" If your book demands illustrations or photographs, forget mass market and think trade paperback or hardcover.

FEE SERVICES

Many unpublished writers think that all agents charge a fee for reading their manuscripts. The vast majority do not but some do, the biggest (and most lucrative) operation being that of the Scott Meredith Literary Agency.

These fee services are pretty much a waste of the author's money, in that the percentage of fee submissions that actually end up getting published is so minute.

One cannot, however, totally discount the value of fee services, for they do offer professional, invariably encouraging, feedback, and for some authors this encouragement alone is worth the price. If you use a fee service, however, you should understand what you are buying.

Fee services are processors of information and they use *generic* criticism personally tailored to your manuscript. So even though the advice you are getting may be legitimately useful, it has been culled from pat phrases and standard responses that have been used to encourage thousands of other would-be authors.

THE BOOKSTORE: GAINING MORE INSIGHT INTO WHAT YOU'RE UP AGAINST

At this point you should have begun to get a feel for your prey, the publisher, and his first line of defense, the editor. You should have gained some insight into how he works, and thinks, what his strengths and weaknesses are, his instincts and habits—and his limitations. To get a better idea of the big picture (and where within that picture you and your book might fit), it is now time to make a trip to your local bookstore.

Though I've been in publishing long enough now so that I should have some idea of what's going on, I make it a point to visit one of the bookstores near my office at least once a week *just to snoop around.* You need to start doing the same thing. Your demeanor should be that of a detective, and your local bookstore should be the scene of the crime. You are looking for clues to help you solve the mysteries of publishing.

Notice the individual subject sections, the space given over to cookbooks say, as opposed to fiction or health and fitness. Usually those sections represent the approximate mix of titles on the average publisher's list.

Interrogate the clerks and *listen* to their answers. "What is your hottest-selling title right now?" "Where are your books on baby and child care?" "Where would I find books by Hemingway or Faulkner?" (This will give you a clue as to how much of the store is given over to back list and how much is devoted to front list.) "What book would you recommend on _____?"

Notice the kinds of books published under different imprints. Which seem to be quality trade paperbacks and which seem to be more popularly oriented?

Form your own insights. What kind of books are displayed spine out as opposed to full cover? What type of book do you see as soon as you walk in the store? How many novels do you see by authors who aren't well known? What *draws* you to pick up certain books and examine them? What books would you pay $15.95 for? What kind of display or promotional material do you notice? What kind of books are sold near the cash register? What seem to be the hottest subject areas? What percentage of the store is devoted to books of local or regional interest?

Pick up books in different formats and examine them. Do any of them "feel" like the book you want to write? Are any of them in the same subject area? Do any of them inspire your own thinking? Notice what formats are common to what types of books.

The bookstore is such an accurate informational microcosm of the publishing industry itself it's sometimes uncanny. Recently, for instance, a client called to say she was disappointed that her second book was not selling that well but was pleased by the resurgence of sales on her first one. I asked her how she happened to know this and she said, "The manager of our local B. Dalton store is a friend, and he told me."

"But that just represents one neighborhood in Seattle," I said.

Later that week I called her publisher to get the sales figures on both books. The editor checked her national computer printouts and said, "The new book is only selling about half as well as the first, but last month we sold more copies of the first book than in any month since publication."

Your local bookstore is your direct link to the New York publishing houses. The savvy aspiring author can figure out more from snooping around there than from reading fifty books on publishing and attending a hundred writers' conferences.

CHAPTER 4
The Awful Truth About Yourself

Now that you have gained some insight into how the publishing industry works (and how it is often amazing that it does), how a publishing house is structured, and, from your bookstore forays, the kind of books publishers seem to be interested in publishing, it is time to get serious. So sit back, relax, take some sodium pentathol, and play a game of truth with yourself.

The bestselling novelist John D. MacDonald once told me that he shuns writers' conferences because, on those occasions when he does rub elbows with his public, he invariably hears the same two comments.

The first is, "Hey, let me give you a great idea for a novel." In so many words, MacDonald politely explains that a successful novelist has far more ideas (the fun part) than the time to write them, and that the last thing he needs is someone else's great ideas.

The second comment is, "Hey, I'm thinking about writing a book myself." This is the one that really gets to him.

"Can you imagine," MacDonald said, "someone going up to Horowitz and saying, 'I've been thinking about giving a concert at Carnegie Hall myself'? Or to Andrew Wyeth: 'I do a little painting every now and then. Who should I approach, the Guggenheim or the Met?'

"Writing for me is a profession," he continued, "but for some reason everyone thinks they should be able to do what I do. I guess it's because everyone writes letters or postcards or laundry lists. So, they figure, why not a book?"

Most successful writers can empathize, painfully, with this observation. For the simple unvarnished truth is that virtually anyone who has read a book thinks he or she ought to be able to write one.

Writing, for the gifted few, is an art, and the chances of reaching this level are about as good as they are of becoming a prima ballerina or a major league second baseman.

Fortunately, however, writing is also a craft and one which can indeed be learned by almost anyone. But even at its craftsman level it is still not something that can be learned overnight, or a skill that pops into your head, fully honed, once you "get around" to putting your publishable thoughts on paper. Even if you aspire to nothing more than to seeing your favorite jokes published, you will at some point have to learn to tell those jokes in print.

On the many occasions when I hear that I've-been-thinking-about-writing-a-book comment, I'm often reminded of a story about the boxer Muhammed Ali, who once found himself involved in a celebrity golf tournament and was asked by a reporter about his aptitude for the game. "I am the greatest golfer who ever lived," Ali replied. "I just haven't played it yet."

As absurd as that may sound, how many would-be authors have told themselves virtually the same thing? "Of course I can write a book; I just haven't gotten around to it yet."

While you don't have to be Hemingway to break into print, even learning to write professionally at the most basic level demands discipline and hard work. The most often repeated cliché about writing is that it is "ten percent inspiration and ninety percent perspiration." I believe an even more apt cliché is "practice makes perfect."

The process can even be compared to becoming a seam-stress or a carpenter. You may know how to sew on a button or hammer a nail, but to make a dress or to build a house you would naturally assume that you would have to figure out a few things, and would then have to keep working at it until you got it right.

The good news is that you probably already know how to drive that nail or sew that button. Most of us have written letters or sales proposals or school compositions—i.e. some-thing that was written for someone else to read.

But writing well—skillfully, professionally—is hard: hard to learn; hard to do; hard to finish once you've started. And in order to do it well, or to do it well enough so that someone might want to publish it, you're going to have to work at it.

Whether your goal is to have one book published or fifty, I think you have to begin by being very honest with yourself. You have to ask yourself certain questions that you might want to pretend don't need an answer.

They do.

Do You Want to Be an "Author" or Do You Want to Write?

An extraordinary mystique has always surrounded the very idea of being an "author." It usually conjures up images of fame and fortune. And people do tend to think of published authors as superior beings, or at least as having something worthwhile to say, even when an author's books are trash.

It is also true that even a single best-seller can become a medium-sized industry and create a small fortune. When Judith Krantz received $3.2 million for the paperback rights to *Princess Daisy*, what with hardcover sales, foreign rights, movie rights, and other commercial spinoffs, even that figure represented only a fraction of what that one book would ultimately earn.

But what many aspiring authors fail to appreciate is that financial success of that magnitude is so unusual that it makes the front page of *The New York Times*. The more realistic expectation is hardly the stuff of dreams, for the average income a book earns for its author is less than $10,000, and the closest most authors ever get to "The Johnny Carson Show" is the TV set in their den.

Writing a book (even a short, "easy" one) is hard enough so that it must be perceived as an end in its own right, rather than the means to the fame and fortune it supposedly is going to bring you.

This question, of course—Do you want to be an author or do you want to write?—is really just a way of getting you to examine your own commitment to writing and to get you to acknowledge that at some point you can't dream or talk your way into print.

As obvious as this is, it is amazing the number of would-be authors who fail to appreciate that books are a medium for writers and not orators, who haven't really thought the process through, and who believe that somehow they are going to be able to finesse the "writing part."

If you haven't made a commitment to write something, don't waste your time dreaming about getting published. You are much better off spending that time trying to come up with the next pet rock.

Is There Anything in Your Experience or Background to Indicate an Aptitude for Writing?

Writing well, like doing anything else well, is something you have to work at. And the simple hard cold fact is that the more you do it the better you are going to get at it.

Diaries, private poetry, and other forms of personal writing don't count. While writing for yourself can be stimulating and definitely rewarding, it is less demanding and less disciplined in form than the kind of writing that is intended for the eyes and judgment of others.

Most creative writing courses, I'm sorry to say, aren't much help either. Their instructors tend to forget that you have to walk before you can run, and that before you can write creatively you must first learn to write uncreatively—i.e. plain, simple sentences which communicate easily understood thoughts.

(In fact, creative writing courses tend to perpetuate the writing mystique—the ghosts of Shakespeare, Dickens, and Faulkner lurking over your shoulder—which becomes one of the greatest inhibiting factors to getting words down on paper. If you can supplant that image of Shakespeare with an image of your average, everyday reader, you will begin to feel less constricted.)

What then does count as training for a writer? Working at one time on your high school or college newspaper, annual, or literary magazine certainly helps, but even this pales in comparison to your competition, the thousands of aspiring authors who write every day as part of their profession (journalists, ad men, copy writers, etc.)

What counts is writing almost every day—learning by doing—and writing something that is meant to be read by others.

Since there is really no place you can go to learn* to write, you are going to have to be inventive:

- Sign on as the editor or writer of a local newsletter or club report.
- Contribute articles to your local shoppers' news.
- Submit pieces to your city magazine or newspaper.

---

*A number of books have been published "on writing well" (in fact, even a very good one written by William Zinsser under that title). The classic, however, is Strunk and White's *The Elements of Style* (MacMillan), a ninety-page gem which proves that brevity is not only the soul of wit but of wisdom. The final chapter, "An Approach to Style," should be memorized.

- Create writing assignments for yourself. (For instance, write out your favorite joke. Now read it aloud to someone. Do you get the same response as you do when you tell it? If not, keep reworking it until you do.)

Do you have an aptitude for writing? Probably. As a very successful author friend once said to me, "If you can talk, you can write." But to paraphrase that old joke: "How do you get to Random House?" "Practice, practice, practice."

Is There Anything in Your Experience or Background That Someone Would Pay $15 to Read About?

As many professional writers would sadly attest, many people think they are doing the author a great favor by just *reading* his or her book. The thought of actually *buying* it would never cross their minds.

Fifteen dollars, the cost of the average hardcover book, is a lot of money for most people to spend. Not only must the buyer want to read your book, he must want to read it pretty badly in order to shell out that much cash, particularly when you consider what that same amount of money could buy: a year's subscription to most magazines, a month of cable television, or even rental of five feature-length films for a VCR. As an author, not only is your book competing against other books, but other forms of comparably priced entertainment as well.

Much of the next chapter will focus on how to create and shape a concept that the buyer will feel is worth $15. It is mentioned here, however, because it is a question that all aspiring authors should keep in mind. Unfortunately, many unpublished writers spend several years completing their autobiographical first novel before it occurs to them.

THE SELF-PUBLISHING ALTERNATIVE

This is a distinguished alternative that has been used by such authors as Mark Twain and Edgar Allan Poe. Many bestsellers started as self-published books, *Mary Ellen's Book of Helpful Hints, The One Minute Manager, How to Flatten Your Stomach, The First Whole Earth Catalogue,* to name just a few. All of these books were privately published and marketed by their authors, and sold well enough to attract the attention of established publishers, who turned them into major books.

Self-publishing is a realistic alternative (and the best way to prove your book's salability), but if you're going to pursue it, it will cost you approximately $4,000 to $5,000 to publish 2,500 copies of a 250-page hardcover book. It is, therefore, advisable to read up on it. For more information here are some books that would be helpful: *The Self-Publishing Handbook* (1985) by David M. Brownstone and Irene M. Franck, published by New American Library (Plume Paperback), 1633 Broadway, New York, NY 10019; $7.95. *The Publish-It-Yourself Handbook* (1980) edited by Bill Henderson, published by the Pushcart Press and Harper and Row, 10 East 53rd Street, New York, NY 10022; $6.95. *How to Publish Your Own Book* (1982) by Lothar W. Mueller, published by Harlo Press, 50 Victor Avenue, Detroit, MI 48203; $5.95.

Are You a Sprinter or a Marathoner?

There is something disheartening about spending a full day producing five perfect pages, only to realize you have 395 more to go. (This is one of the reasons professional writers often get depressed.)

Writing books is usually not for those who demand instant gratification. The process, by nature, is slow, a couple of months for a publisher to make a decision on your proposal or manuscript, a year of writing, and another twelve months for the publisher to publish—almost two and a half years from start to finished books.

What other tasks have you completed where you knew, even before you began, that the entire process was going to take two and a half years? Are you good at finishing what you start, even when "the light at the end of the tunnel" looks like Betelgeuse?

In summary, there are no awful truths about yourself and your potential relationship with the publishing world that can't be overcome. But in writing a book, more than in almost any endeavor you can think of, the proof is in the pudding. There is no place to run or hide. You can't fake it. If you are not willing to face these truths you have only two choices: abandon your book idea altogether—or hire a ghost writer.

SECTION II

Taming a Wild Idea

CHAPTER 5
So What Should I Write About?

A n idea is the brain's most perishable commodity. When criticized or discouraged, it spoils quickly. Or, if it lingers too long without becoming something more substantial, it grows stale or gradually evaporates.

To start to make a book idea real, and to give it enough steam to overcome inertia, I think you have to begin by thinking of it as real—as a tangible *product*—and of yourself as a salesman bringing it to market.

Fortunately, this is the one aspect of the publishing business that works for you rather than against you. All books obviously start out as ideas, and as far as publishers are concerned the right book ideas are "products."

This is not an exaggeration. Publishers have been known to commit to a book on the strength of a half-page concept or, even occasionally, on nothing more than a wonderful title. Indeed, it is much more common for publishers to pay for an idea which has been effectively presented in a well thought out proposal than for a completed manuscript.

Moreover, publishers are so aggressive and so highly competitive in acquiring good book ideas that historically even in the worst of times for the industry, for the right idea, it is *always* a seller's market.

51

There is, of course, one catch: your idea must be salable. It must appeal to a broad readership and be focused to that readership in such a way so as to make it special or unique. Much of the middle section of this book, in fact, is devoted to showing you how to recognize a good salable idea when you see one and how to turn it into something even better.

For the moment, however, a good way to begin to understand what constitutes a salable idea is to come at it from the publisher's perspective, and to examine the kinds of books that they have traditionally acquired. For as any experienced salesman will tell you, one of the first rules of selling is to find out what the buyer is looking to buy.

THE PUBLISHER'S LIST

Publishers, of course, do not arbitrarily decide to acquire this title and reject that one. And while certain publishers may specialize, they are all in their own way seeking to accommodate the varied tastes and differing appetites of the book-buying public.

Book buyers, often to the consternation of publishers, can be just as fickle as any other buyers. Yet over the years certain unwritten general guidelines have emerged as to types of books readers most commonly prefer and the quantities in which they prefer them. Obviously, these reader preferences help predetermine the mix of titles on a publisher's list.

Cookbooks, for instance, will always be published because there will always be a market for them. On the other hand, cookbooks will never outdistance fiction in popularity. If you go into almost any bookstore, you will see that the relative space given over to these two categories will reflect this reader preference reality.

As times and tastes change, certain types of books do surge forward with a vengeance—business books are a good recent example—then recede into the background as times and tastes change again. Publishers, of course, respond to these ebbs and flows in the marketplace in terms of the titles they select, which is why the rules governing what publishers are looking to publish are anything but hard and fast.

Still, there are perennial types of books which fall quite naturally into certain groupings, and a practical analysis of these groupings should be useful to the aspiring author/salesman. Each grouping is analyzed here in terms of the opportunity it presents to the unpublished writer and the aptitude that each may require.

How-To Books

The words "how-to" immediately conjure up a negative image of books on knitting or boating. Generally, however, it's the largest category of books in all of publishing, and unquestionably the most successful one. It is also the most fertile field for new, unique, salable ideas and creative twists on old ones and therein lies one of your best clues as to the ballpark you might be thinking about playing in.

Bestsellers such as *Jane Fonda's Workout Book,* the real estate investment guide *Nothing Down,* even diet books are every bit as much how-to books as those that show you how to knit one/purl two or cast off.

I would even consider certain informational books to fall within this grouping. *The People's Pharmacy,* for instance, a bestseller of several years ago, which provided much-needed information about over-the-counter drugs, was very much a how-to book ("how to" buy these drugs by knowing what you are buying) though the how-to was unstated—subliminal.

How-to is the classic find-a-need-and-fill-it category, which is what makes it such a fertile area. The public is always coming up with some new need—some new craving for new information—which it is looking for someone to fill.

It is also an area where one can be the most inventive. *Total Fitness in Thirty Minutes a Week* and *The One Minute Manager,* for instance, are good examples of books where their authors grafted a desirable get-it-over-with element onto a conventional type of book. As a result, they came up with bestselling titles which far outdistanced the more traditional books on fitness and management.

It should be mentioned that how-to books, as broadly defined here, might encompass up to thirty to thirty-five sections of a bookstore—health, business, fitness, finance, travel, baby care, etc. But as "official" publishing terminology it carries with it a much more narrow connotation (knitting and boating books, for instance) and is often used to refer to modest back-listed books on hobbies and specialized interests. Therefore, while almost half of all non-fiction books published will fall under this broad-based definition, do *not* characterize your own proposed book as such ("This is a how-to book on . . .") in your submission.

Cookbooks

Cookbooks are obviously another type of how-to, but they are treated separately here because so many people have thought about writing one.

More cookbooks are published annually than any other type of book. Yet this is a brand name business dominated by the Julia Childs, James Beards and "Betty Crockers" of the world, and the magazines that service the woman's market, such as *Good Housekeeping* and *Woman's Day*. (One woman, desperate to get her cookbook published, once told me she was even willing to change her last name to Betterhomesandgardens.)

Your best bet is to concentrate on regional or specialty cooking that may not, as yet, have had its day in the sun. Many of the successful specialty cookbooks have been geared to whatever the hot, new specialty appliance happens to be. Here, it's usually the firstest with the mostest. Several years ago a woman by the name of Mable Hoffman wrote a cookbook entitled *Crockery Cookery*. It sold over a million copies. Recent hot appliances have been the wok, the food processor, and the microwave oven. Recent hot regional specialty cuisines have been Cajun and Tex/Mex.

Hopes and Dreams Books

Also called "armchair" books, these acknowledge the simple fact that people like to experience life vicariously. When people buy *Architectural Digest*, for instance, it's not because they're planning to become decorators or because they're going to buy one of the homes in the magazine. It's because they like to "visit" these homes and imagine what it's like to live among such luxurious surroundings. Many books that you might not expect fall into this category.

Eugene Fodor, author of the *Fodor Travel Guides*, once told me a story that illustrates the unusual book form in which vicarious entertainment can sometimes be delivered.

He had published a basic travel guide to India and, surprisingly, it had its biggest worldwide sales in Hungary. Why did a book on India do so well with readers who had no hope of ever getting there? Precisely because it was so exotic, so unattainable, Fodor surmised. Just to be able to read about restaurants and hotel accommodations was fantasy fulfillment for all those readers locked in gray Hungary.

Many luxuriant, copiously illustrated coffee table books fall into this category as do certain "up-market" travel books such as *The Sophisticated Traveller* and *The Great Railway Bazaar*, or even *Road Food*, where the authors travelled around the United States eating at different restaurants and then writing about their experiences for the rest of us.

You should consider submitting something in this category only if you can devise a book that does not demand color reproductions.

Autobiographies and Biographies

The sad, simple truth is that even if you have led a full and fascinating life, unless you're famous, no one really wants to read about you. So if you're really serious about getting published, and you're neither famous nor the offspring of someone famous (and bursting to tell nasty stories about mom or dad), you should be aware that you are fighting an uphill battle, and the hill is Mt. Rushmore.

There are many interesting lives whose stories are still waiting to be told, so biographies are a worthwhile avenue to explore. They can range in scope and length from a quickie "fan" book on a hot rock or movie superstar to a more ambitious effort such as *Son of the Morningstar,* the bestseller on the life of General George Armstrong Custer.

Even when considering biographies, you have to be realistic. Frank Sinatra's life is a good story, but keep in mind that he's not going to ask you to help him write his autobiography, and to do his biography without his consent requires access to a lot of people who aren't going to give it to you. For this reason biographies of historical figures or of people who were unusual and fascinating "footnotes" to history are probably your best bet.

Inspirational/Motivational/Self-Help Books

These how-to books can be thought of as "how to be happier" books because they cover qualitative things such as how to like yourself, or how to get along better with your husband, wife, child, dog . . . whomever.

Although certain kinds of inspirational/motivational books go in and out of vogue, there's always a need for them. Just take a look at any recent bestseller list and you will usually find at least one or two. Check the bestseller list regularly over a period of time and you will see how the pendulum swings back and forth with these books. For example, it's pretty unlikely that you'll find a book like *Winning Through Intimidation* on the same list with *How to Be Your Own Best Friend.* The first is "hard" self-help (get them before they get you); the second is softer, gentler, more empathetic. The tone and approach of these books generally reflect whatever national angst we happen to be experiencing.

As salable as these books sometimes are, keep in mind that they often demand the involvement of a credentialled expert—a psychiatrist, nutritionist, or therapist—as coauthor to lend the book credibility.

Pop Syndrome/Pop Theory Books

A related category of books that are written by "experts" are those which seek to popularize certain sociological and psychological theories. *The Peter Pan Syndrome* and *The Culture of Narcissism* are examples of the type. These books are often written by academicians who have recast their subjects to have wider popular appeal.

Investigative Books

It's better to leave these to professional journalists, though the potential here for qualified writers is enormous. *Wired, Fatal Vision, Blood and Money,* and *All the President's Men* are all bestselling examples of this category.

There's a big mistake that many journalists make when they first try their hand at these books: they forget that they can't be done for the sensationalism alone. They have to have some significance beyond the actual story itself. Norman Mailer, for instance, wrote *The Executioner's Song* about the *first* man to die when capital punishment was reintroduced, not the second, third, or fourth.

Children's Books

Many first-time authors attempt children's books because they think it is one of the easier forms of writing. In fact, it is one of the hardest. Normally, the shape these never-to-be-published stories take is a simplistic, and often simple-minded, tale that ends with a moral.

Children *hate* blatant moralizing. They love books because they allow them to escape into a world of fantasy, and an obvious moral at the end of a story only serves to jerk them back to the world of reality. Read the bestselling authors in this genre, Maurice Sendak or Dr. Seuss, for instance, and you will see these books are often dominated by naughty, even mean, little characters.

The best children's books are those that appeal not just to children but to the child in everyone.

It should also be noted that books for young people include "Y.A." or "young adult" titles. As with adult authors, the best—Judy Blume, Paul Zindel, or Robert Cormier—are in a class by themselves. However, some of the more formulaic young adult series have become a category of fiction and do represent something of an opportunity for first-time authors.

Humor Books

This category also includes gimmick and "non-book" books such as *Real Men Don't Eat Quiche* and many of the books that feature lots of silly lists, few words on a page, or have something sticking out of them.

This is one of those categories that publishers have saturated and are now in the process of killing. In the wake of some genuinely clever books (*The Preppie Handbook,* for instance) that came out several years ago, publishers rushed

in to destroy millions of trees by printing the most extraordinary array of unfunny "humor books" imaginable.

Today, as a result of these failures, the humor market is
dominated almost totally by cartoon characters and licensed
brand names such as Garfield, Doonesbury, and Bloom
County. If you are syndicated in fewer than 700 newspapers
your chances of getting anything published in this genre are
very slim.

There are two other "problems" with humor books. One is
that humor is like reality: everyone has his or her own
version of what it is. Rare is the writer who can simultaneously
tickle a mass number of funny bones.

The other problem is that being able to write genuinely
funny is probably even more difficult than being able to write
genuinely well. Throughout history there may have been
maybe a thousand brilliantly funny writers.

If you insist, do not start off your proposal by saying, "This
is a humorous book about . . ." That's like telling someone
how funny a joke is going to be just before you tell it. In the
rare instance that you are a genuinely funny writer let the
editor discover this for him or herself.

Fiction

You probably can't write fiction because very few people can.
Still, I don't expect that statement to dissuade a single soul,
for almost anyone who is committed to writing fiction is
already convinced that he or she will fall within this select
group of the gifted.

Though commercial fiction may not always be an art, it is
certainly a very special craft. Many frustrated writers rationalize that their fiction is too "literary"—i.e. too good—for
the marketplace. That's an excuse for not being able to tell a
good story.

Unfortunately, there is almost no way to judge if you are a

latent fiction talent who simply hasn't been discovered yet. On the plus side, however, writing publishable fiction does not require an I.Q. of a genius. It also does not seem to demand a particular professional background: Colleen McCullough, before she wrote *The Thornbirds*, was a nurse; Rosemary Rogers, a secretary; Judith Krantz, an ad agency exec; and Judith Guest, a housewife.

It does demand aptitude, or, at the very least, the ability to "run a movie inside your head," an intuitive story sense that plays out scene by scene. An understanding of human nature (characterization, motivation, and so forth) also doesn't hurt.

Not surprising, a number of actors (a profession that combines intuition, training, and seeing movies on paper) have made the successful transition to bestselling novelists, including Tom Tryon, Robert Ludlum, and Jacqueline Susann. Less surprising, Sidney Sheldon, William Goldman, and Mario Puzo have all been successful screenwriters as well as novelists.

If you are serious about writing fiction the best way to begin is to postpone thinking about serious fiction. Today, even critically acclaimed novelists are finding it difficult to get their next book published. Instead, figure out how the commercial big leaguers do it, write a blockbuster, then slip in the serious book you really want to write on its coattails.

If you are determined to write serious fiction only and are loath to first try your hand at more commercial fare, then you should be aware that all the dire warnings you've heard are not exaggerated.

On the off chance that you are the next Joyce Carol Oates or John Updike, concentrate first on publication in literary reviews and quarterlies or in magazines that publish serious fiction. This will give you credibility that is otherwise difficult to come by and will make the perilous path you have chosen for yourself ever so slightly easier to navigate.

The only other serious fiction option is to find a respected sponsor. The story of the posthumous publication of John

Kennedy Toole's Pulitzer Prize–winning *Confederacy of Dunces*, of how it was repeatedly rejected until Walker Percy recognized its merits and recommended its publication, is now publishing legend. But the sad truth is that if Percy had not stepped in, Toole's small masterpiece, to this day, probably would have remained unpublished.

Assuming that you do have some latent commercial fiction talent, the key to writing publishable novels is to study that fiction which has recently been published.

Analyze the "category books" such as romance, mystery, and science fiction, written by the biggest names in their fields. Try to intuit the conventions of the genre. How do the big names "play" with these conventions? Take notes!

Study the bestsellers. How, for instance, do these authors manage to make you keep turning pages? Rate the various novelistic elements in terms of their bestselling importance: characterization; theme; pacing; plot; dialogue; texture; voice; setting; suspension of disbelief. What determines chapters? Do they begin and end indiscriminately, or do they often leave you hanging and pick up the next chapter with a different character or subplot?

Robin Cook, a doctor, and author of *Coma* and several other bestsellers, said that once he had decided to write fiction, he began by reading a hundred bestselling novels, one after the next, before writing a single word.

The best course on "Writing Fiction for Publication" that you will ever find, you can design for yourself right from your local bookstore.

Amalgams

As a final thought on the groupings in this chapter, it is worth reiterating that they should neither be thought of as official publishing categories nor as pigeonholes in which book ideas can be neatly stuck. Many books, in fact, are often an amalgam of several of these groupings. A diet book for instance could be 1) a cookbook, 2) a motivational book, and 3) a how-to book, all at once.

A perfect example of a book that amalgamates, perhaps even transcends, some of the above categories is the bestseller *Iacocca.* While it is obviously an autobiography, it is also a how-to, because you can learn something about business from it. But, primarily, it is inspirational because the book is a classic Horatio Alger rags-to-riches story. The amalgam here is a potent one—so potent that Iacocca's autobiography is one of the bestselling books of all time.

CHAPTER 6
The Click of a Good Idea

Over the past fifty years the book publishing business has undergone a gradual evolution. There was a time when publishers were as likely to perceive books as a forum for new ideas and independent thought as they were a means of commerce.

But to combat the always dismal economics of the business, publishers have been forced to become more reactive, and today, like network television, what publishers choose to publish is more a reflection of our culture than an influence upon it. This is not a judgment, just a fact, which anyone can glean from looking at any recent bestseller list.

What this means to you is that what publishers are most interested in publishing is hardly a closely guarded secret. In fact, it is all around you. It is a matter of analyzing popular trends, figuring out what people are interested in, and intuiting what they are on the verge of caring about next.

While one can't "learn" to be intuitive, there is a systematic way to go about exposing your intuition to the right stimuli and developing the mind-set that allows you to know a good book idea when you hear or see one.

THE "PURITY" OF A GOOD IDEA

When you are sifting ideas around, it is best to begin by assuming that you have no limitations at all. Be open to anything.

Of course, at some point you will have to be realistic. If the book idea you come up with involves collaboration with Henry Kissinger, it is probably an idea that won't come to fruition. Nevertheless, the better your idea, the better your chances are of attracting the people you need to help you execute it. If your best approach is a collaboration with someone with recognized expertise in a particular field, the quicker that person is able to grasp your idea's potential, the greater your chances of eliciting his or her support. People are attracted to good ideas like moths to a flame. Good ideas open doors.

START WITH WHAT YOU KNOW— BUT DON'T STOP THERE

The former editorial director of a paperback house once told me of being chastised by an agent for rejecting an autobiographical novel that was so bad it should never have been submitted in the first place:

"You know what they say," the agent said, "everyone has at least one book in them."

"Yes," my friend said, "but I don't have to publish it."

The lesson of that exchange is that yes, you probably do have a book in you, but you better figure out if it is one someone might want to publish.

One of the pieces of advice that is often handed out to aspiring writers is "write what you know." That's a good place to begin but don't stop there. The majority of books published are less about what the writer "knew" than what he or she was anxious to learn, a subject that sparked his or her own curiosity.

What Is Your Passion?

One of the great attractions of writing professionally is that it allows you to indulge your passions, to drop in on an unfamiliar world for a year or two and then move on to another, to become, in a way, a professional dilettante.

Over the years I have had many conversations with writers who were stumped on what their next book should be. To get them off the dime I have often found it helpful to explore with them some of their passions other than writing—subjects and areas of interest which they had dismissed as hobbies or had assumed were of interest only to them.

It is surprising how often these brainstorming sessions have led directly to published books: a book on house plants by a science fiction writer; a unique family-style cookbook by a well-known humorist; a book on organizing by a writer and self-described "born slob" who had finally discovered a system that worked for her.

One writer I know, a great baseball fan, recently had the opportunity to ghostwrite the autobiography of a famous baseball player. He was more a fan than an expert when he began, and he certainly wasn't willing to trade in his typewriter for a job in the team's front office when he finished. But for one season he got to experience baseball as an "insider," to indulge one of his great passions. As a result, he probably wrote a better book than if the same assignment had been handed to a jaded sportswriter who was part of that world every day.

The best advice to an aspiring writer may not be "write what you know" but "write what you want to know more about." Explore the outer limits of your curiosity; feel around the fringes of your interests; indulge yourself. If you find something that secretly fascinates you, you may find that it fascinates many others as well.

Here are some leading questions you might want to ask yourself:

- What am I really passionate about?
- What do I always wish I had more time for?
- If I had a year to be a "professional dilettante," how would I spend it?
- What do I often think about when I'm alone and deep in conversation with myself?
- What do I worry about? What issues, events, and trends concern me the most?
- What have I done, or what experience have I had, that people seem curious about?
- Is there any topic on which friends invariably turn to me for advice?

The book you may *think* you have "in you" may not be publishable no matter how well you present it. But people are not one-dimensional, and you probably have the germ of many books worthy of publication, if not in you, at least within your domain. It is often simply a matter of opening yourself up to the possibilities.

TUNING IN

A lot of people in publishing, and certainly most writers, have developed a kind of sixth sense as to what makes a book, and their antennae are out all the time.

Usually, this is not a conscious process: A writer will be quickly scanning the *Wall Street Journal*, primarily to check out the one stock he owns. His eye catches a small item, maybe just a filler, about a stockbroker in Texas who is outperforming all the so-called experts on Wall Street.

That night in the shower, or maybe the next day walking down the street, that item about the broker comes back to him. His mind begins to make connections: Texas equals money and the best stockbroker in the country lives in Dallas. "Hmm," he says to himself, *The Texas Investment Guide.* Maybe I should get in touch with that guy."

Though perhaps not the world's greatest example, the above does illustrate how the tuning-in process works: the news item was read at two levels. Consciously, it was absorbed as information; subconsciously, it was scrutinized for the seeds of a salable book.

Having now been immersed in publishing for over a decade I find I can't read the side of a cereal box without subconsciously asking myself "Is there a book in it?" (*The Brand Name Calorie Counter,* after all, did sell over a million copies. I wonder if its author was inspired by her box of Kellogg's Cornflakes?)

This sixth sense—absorbing information at two levels for dual purposes—is hardly a trait unique to the publishing community. Have you ever noticed, for instance, how a news item relating to your own job or work will catch your eye, even though you are not consciously thinking about work, and even under the most incongruous circumstances? That is your own informational sixth sense in action. The only difference, perhaps, is that for professional book people, *everything* is work-related, everything from the hot new rock group to tax reform.

Most people who gravitate to publishing, writers and editors both, seem to have a good general knowledge of the world and the culture around them. They actually *enjoy* waiting in a dentist's office, because it gives them a chance to flip through several magazines they might not otherwise see. They are naturally curious and, again, that relationship between curiosity and the click of an idea cannot be overemphasized.

But converting "raw data" into salable book ideas takes more than curiosity. It demands consciously looking out for them and actively bombarding your mind with a Chinese menu of stimuli—opening yourself up to the world around you.

Your subconscious will very often do the rest, but only once you have actively and aggressively put yourself into the hunt.

Resource Material

"Tuning in" naturally brings up the question: what should you be tuning in to? What source material is most likely to yield the germ of a good book idea?

The most obvious answer is anything and everything. There are, however, certain publications, other media, and areas of general interest which have historically generated more books than others.

Popular Magazines. "Popular" here means "pop," those magazines which rely on provocative articles heralded by strong copy lines on the cover to attract a mostly newsstand (as opposed to subscription) audience. Most of the women's magazines—from *Cosmopolitan* to *Glamour* to *Woman's Day*— fall within this category. The all-time champion is *People*. Every year, ten to twenty new books are generated from its pages. "Bellwether" magazines, from the popular (*Omni*) to the serious (*Scientific American*), are also good source material.

Pop News Shows. These are the "infor-tainment" shows such as "60 Minutes," "Good Morning America," "20/20," "The Today Show," "Entertainment Tonight," and certain news specials. The program content of these shows tends to focus on popular trends, newsmakers, and the issues that most Americans are concerned about. "The Donahue Show" is perhaps the best at taking America's pulse. The problem, however, is that it usually features guests who have already written books on the issues it covers. One might do pretty well simply by following a Donahue lead on those shows where his guests haven't written books.

Newspapers. *The New York Times* generates more stories and items that become books than any other publication. This is less the result of the *Times* being exceptionally in tune with the times, than it is the result of geography. Since most trade publishers are located in New York, it ends up being the newspaper that most publishing people read.

Next in line would be the national newspapers: *The Wall Street Journal, The Christian Science Monitor,* and *USA Today.*

There is also a lot to be said for your local newspaper. Many feature stories that might interest you are usually sent over the wire services—AP, UPI, Gannett—and are picked up by most local papers. Additionally, local items which have the potential to generate national interest appear in most metropolitan newspapers with some regularity.

Books out of news items, by the way, are rarely found on the front page or generated out of the headlines. They are much more likely to be found in the paper's feature sections— the "living" and "style" sections, the women's page, the sports page.

In scouring the print media, newspapers or magazines, you must constantly be asking yourself, "What caught my eye?" "What story grabbed me and didn't let go?" If it grabbed you, it may grab a lot of other people as well.

Social Anthropology. It is important to distinguish pop trends—society's ephemera—from real trends, or cultural change. Both generate books, but pop trends (Rubik's Cube, Valley Girls, Trivial Pursuit) are like quicksilver, easy to spot but quickly gone. If you nail one at the right moment (timing is critical—too early is as bad as too late) your book has major-league potential. But hitting one on the nose is more luck than design.

The real or more substantive trends not only represent the

present but the near future. Women's issues, the baby boom, the graying of America, career obsession, and even preoccupation with the future itself are all examples of recent cultural trends that will be around for some time. Hundreds of books in these areas will be published over the next decade.

Bestseller Lists. Recently, I saw an interview in a national magazine with one of New York's most successful book packagers. When asked about his success—how he had generated ideas for over 200 published books in less than five years—he said, "We don't have to be geniuses . . . we merely look at the bestseller list."

Read between the lines of bestseller lists. They are not only a statistical analysis, but a reflection of national tastes and interests, and, by extension, a sound indication of what books publishers are currently most interested in publishing. For instance, when a book entitled *How to Make Love to a Man* reached the upper rungs of the bestseller list, was it any wonder that a book entitled *How to Make Love to a Woman* soon followed?

Naturally, however, you must consider the normal delay between submission and publication. If, for instance, several books in the same subject area are currently residing on the bestseller list, you can assume that a glut of related titles will soon follow, and that a purely derivative idea is not going to stand much of a chance. But bestseller lists are also an indication of emerging interests and new trends. The idea is not to copy what is already on the bestseller list, but to allow it to act as a mental springboard and to suggest the kinds of books that may be there in a year.

What This Country Needs... I wasn't around when Thomas Marshall promoted the need for a good five-cent cigar, and there probably wasn't "a book in it" anyway. But I have found that listening to what people say—listening to their concerns, their interests, their fears, their frustrations,

PUBLISHERS WEEKLY

Of the many publications that purport to serve the publishing industry, the one that actually does is *Publishers Weekly. Publishers Weekly* (known as *PW*) is the industry's trade magazine, and is as indispensable to the publishing community as *Advertising Age* is to the advertising industry.

A *PW* subscription is expensive ($78 a year for 51 issues), but almost all libraries subscribe and make it available to those who ask.

PW reflects and even shapes the thinking of the book publishing industry. There are a number of features and columns in the magazine, but the ones that will be most helpful to you in getting a better grasp of the industry are: News of the Week; Trade News; Bookselling and Merchandising; the bestseller list, and, of course, the ads and the new title announcements. The Spring Announcements and Fall Announcements issues, published every February and August, and the ABA (American Bookseller Association) Convention issue, published every June, are of particular interest to aspiring authors.

really listening to what they want to talk about, what really turns them on—to be a consistent source of inspiration for book ideas.

Is the extraordinary success of *Nothing Down* a big surprise? When was the last time you attended a cocktail party where someone *didn't* bring up real estate? With tax reform now inevitable, do you think this is an issue that will concern (and confuse) many people? Once it passes Congress, watch publishers' lists for an answer.

TIMING

In 1976, Jim Fixx wrote and published *The Complete Book of Running*. Fixx happened to catch the jogging craze just as it was beginning to crest, and as a result his book went on to sell over two million copies and to become one of the bestselling how-to books of all time.

However, one of publishing's peculiarities is that if that exact same book had been published two years earlier or two years later it would have achieved only a small fraction of its success.

The role timing plays in the salability of your idea is probably already self-evident. The more "pop" your idea is, for instance, the quicker it is likely to become "unpop." Similarly, while bestseller lists and cocktail party chatter are valid measurements of a current rage, how quickly does this information become old news?

Moreover, being too far ahead of your time is just as bad as being too late. Publishers do not like to play guessing games, and unless you can marshal an extraordinary amount of evidence to support the timeliness of your concept, they would just as well have someone else take the risk. (Second-man-in is not so spectacular, but it's a lot safer.)

The key is to spot a new trend (or a shift in direction of an old one) just as it is emerging—as it is gaining momentum rather than as it is starting to lose it. Fortunately, it's not as difficult as it may sound.

Emerging popular and social trends do not come and go with the season. Even the trendiest of topics stays around for a year or two. Others will last for a generation. And some, such as our universal pursuit of happiness, will go on forever, though the form in which these perennial trends disguise themselves often changes from year to year.

Naturally, however, your ability to spot new trends, new

ideas, and emerging interests in a timely manner is strictly a function of how tuned in you are to the world around you. And these timely new ideas, many of which will end up on bestseller lists, are just as accessible to you as they are to anyone else.

CHAPTER 7
Getting Serious

L et's suppose that you now know what you want to write about, or that you already knew even before you picked up this book. Now it's time to get to the nitty-gritty, and write your proposal, right?

Wrong. And wrong for two reasons.

First, your idea is going to have to pass muster. You are going to have to subject it to certain criteria, and examine the results with clear-eyed objectivity. There is nothing worse than committing a lot of time and effort to a proposal only to find out that almost the exact same book was published six months earlier (I know, because I've done it) or to discover, after fifteen rejections, that there are only 700 other people on the entire planet who share your passion for collecting colored aluminum foil.

Second, the idea you commit to a proposal will, or should be, quite different from the one that exists in its original, pristine form. It needs to germinate. It is not until you have explored all its possibilities, mutations, and tangents—even wrong ones—that your idea can be seen in its best possible light and really begin to take shape.

The process of converting an idea into a book proposal is

almost an exact replica of writing a book itself: research; germination; and execution.

The bestselling author Gay Talese has talked about his own germination process. After he has finished his research and interviewing for a book, it will take him months before he can actually begin work on the manuscript. During this period he will type and retype his notes, transcribe and retranscribe his interviews, index and cross-index files, and intricately label all with a rainbow of colored pencils.

What he is really doing, of course, is allowing his ideas about the book to germinate. By indexing and cross-indexing his notes and interviews, he is in the process of not only absorbing them but of possessing them. By the time he begins to write they exist in his mind, symbiotic with and indistinguishable from his own thoughts on the subject.

Taking an idea to the proposal stage is a microcosm of this process. It is only when you have explored your idea in all its many forms that you can even begin to get the best form down on paper.

From my own experience as a book packager I have come to learn that my initial book idea invariably evolves into something quite different by the time it reaches the proposal. I have also come to learn that here "different" is almost always better.

Additionally, the more I find myself thinking through an idea, or merely thinking about it, the more real it becomes to me. And once I have given the idea enough thought, and allowed it enough time to mature and ripen, I find the proposal practically writes itself.

There is, however, one caution. An idea is most fragile while it is germinating. Too short and you shortchange the idea; too long and you kill the muse. Moreover, it is the stage when you are more vulnerable to talking yourself out of the project, or to pretending to ponder when you are really procrastinating.

The key, as Gay Talese's methodology illustrates, is to

make germination active rather than passive. An idea must be nurtured in order to grow. Seek out information. Read up on your idea and think actively about it—in the shower, while driving, during TV commercials. You will be amazed at the possibilities that your initial idea begins to suggest and the new excitement this inspires.

GETTING TO KNOW YOUR READER

Earlier I touched upon the importance of a writer knowing his or her readers ("the reader over your shoulder"), which should give clues about communication, style, and the voice the writer should be using in "speaking" to them. Similarly, one of the most fruitful ways to think creatively about your idea is to begin to come at it from the reader's perspective.

A book, of course, is a two-way proposition, an intersecting of the knowledge of the writer, or his or her ability to entertain, with a desire for that knowledge or entertainment on the part of the reader. Even the most brilliantly rendered book is not going to sell if the subject matter does not engage its readers and draw them in. Engaging your reader is not something that begins with the writing of the manuscript, but with the formulation of the idea itself.

Coming at your idea from the reader's point of view is role reversal in its most artful, insightful form, for what you are trying to do is get beneath the surface, to find out how your reader *feels* even more than how he or she thinks.

Take diet books, for instance, which are bought over and over again by the same people. While a woman who has bought the last ten bestselling diet books may be consciously aware that she has bought the tenth because the first nine didn't work—and may feel a little silly about it—her desire to lose weight is so great (and reinforced every time she looks at a fashion magazine) that her logical self is all but consumed by her burning fantasy of being thin.

Once you get beneath the surface and begin to understand the *subliminal motivation* a reader has in buying your book, this will suggest crucial nuances and subtleties to your idea that simply will not occur to you otherwise.

So what do you do? Stop ten people on the corner and ask, "Are you my reader?"? Even if this were practical, what you would get would be opinions rather than feelings, and probably ten different opinions at that. Yet as different and individualistic as people like to think they are, what is really amazing is how much they are all alike.

Talk to a parent about his or her child, for instance, and the commonality of feeling, the parent's love and hopes for that child, is almost universal. Hold up a family heirloom and announce that you are going to sell it. What kind of emotional response would that provoke, and how common do you think that response might be?

Books that sell well invariably touch a common nerve. They *link* their audience at some subliminal level. This can range from the poignant (*Good Morning, Merry Sunshine* sensitively captured a father's love for a child) to the not-so-poignant (*Jane Fonda's Workout* conveys the message that women want to look like Jane Fonda) to the ridiculous (*Thin Thighs in 30 Days* equals "I'll solve my lifelong cellulite problem in a month").

Many books on parenting, for instance, while offering straightforward advice (such as "Dr. Spock") actually serve a more subliminal fundamental purpose of reassuring parents and quelling their natural fears. Even if these books are seldom read, and simply sit on a nearby shelf, they become, for the parents, a kind of security blanket between book covers.

Look for the subliminal feelings that would motivate readers to be drawn to your book. For once you find them, you will gain more insight into your ideas than you probably will from hundreds of hours of research.

QUESTIONS ABOUT YOUR READERS

The danger in trying to get to know your readers is that you might find that they don't like your book, or worse, that they don't even exist.

What should happen, however, is that once you bring in the reader's perspective, you will be forced to become more objective about your own idea, which, in turn, should lead to a reshaping and a more targeted focusing of your original concept.

To gain this perspective, you are going to have to ask yourself some hard questions about your potential readers, and (even harder) answer them truthfully. If your idea doesn't pass muster at this stage, if you can't justify it in terms of its potential audience or come up with an approach that will satisfy that audience, then any further effort may well be a waste of time.

How Many Readers Do You Have? Begin to quantify your audience as soon as possible. You may want this information for your proposal anyway, but first and foremost it will tell you a lot about exactly where your idea stands.

How many potential readers do you have? Remember, book distribution is at best a scattershot process and any one book is probably competing with others on the same subject for the reader's loyalty. If your audience is not that big to begin with, it is simply going to be lost in the shuffle.

If your potential audience is less than two to three million, reaching them through bookstores becomes problematic. An audience significantly smaller than that is simply too small and too diffuse to be found through normal book-selling channels.

On a more encouraging note, when quantifying your audience, don't forget to add in the "pass through" factor. A career or job hunting guide, for instance, would appeal primarily to an audience of only 2.5 million graduating college seniors. However, this audience not only grows slightly every year, it also totally regenerates itself. Every year another two to three million college graduates "pass through" a need for a career guide. The potential audience for certain career guides is therefore a lot larger than it might at first seem.

Also seek out any other evidence that helps define your audience. Several years ago, for instance, I was working on a book with a popular television chef. One day he just happened to mention to me that whenever he demonstrated a recipe that featured chicken or apples his recipe requests from viewers tripled. Naturally, his completed book featured quite a few chicken and apple recipes.

Figures about a potential audience can also be helpful in suggesting ideas. If, for instance, you come across an article stating that bicycle sales have risen dramatically in the past year, that might suggest that books on bicycling will soon rise in popularity as well.

If you are passionate enough to want to write about a certain subject, you probably already have some sense as to the size of your potential audience or at least where to go to get that information. If not, a good place to begin is your local library. An inquiry there most likely will not elicit the answers you are seeking but you will probably get some good clues—phone numbers and addresses of service organizations, information bureaus, and government agencies which specialize in statistics and numbers of this sort.

Where Do They Live? Books of strong regional or local interest can still be quite successful even if their potential audience is less than two million, the obvious reason being that most of the audience is located in one place and is therefore easy to reach. These books, a local guidebook, for instance, or a regional cookbook, would naturally be most attractive to a local or regional publisher.

On the other hand, a book that appeals to every living

soul in and around Tulsa, Oklahoma, but nowhere else, is not likely to attract the attention of a New York publisher. Don't forget the awful reality of all those books that are being published. A regional book, by virtue of being region- al, demands too much special time and attention.

Generally, the more national your audience is in scope, the more receptive a publisher is going to be. The upside potential is greater and a publisher with a national sales force to feed would just as soon sell one hundred copies of a book in each state as he would five thousand copies only in Oklahoma.

Are They Passionate? The "passion quotient" of your audience is a major factor in sizing up your idea's salability and appeal.

Tennis players and skiers, for instance, prefer participating to reading books on their particular sports. While books on these subjects perform fairly well, they are only modestly successful in relation to the actual number of tennis players and skiers in the United States.

On the other hand, the audiences for books on military history, sailing, opera, and dance are small but passionate. They voraciously devour almost any quality book that is published in their particular area.

Do They Buy Books? Aah, here's a problem. Do they buy books? Do they even go into book stores?

Auto racing, for instance—Indy cars, stock cars, drag racing, etc. combined—attracts more spectators than any other sport, over sixty million annually. Unfortunately, only a few thousand of them ever go into bookstores, and books on auto racing have never fared well as a result.

Unfortunately, accurate information about the consumer's book-buying habits is hard to come by. Surveys, for instance, have historically proven to be unreliable. Next to sex, the subject people are most likely to lie about in surveys is their reading habits, and I have seen some surveys which, if they could be taken seriously, would make book publishing just slightly larger than the automobile industry.

Many years ago, I did see a poll which claimed to be an accurate survey of book-reading and book-buying habits, in that it was supposedly disguised to survey something else. The depressing statistics were that only 35 percent of Americans had read a book since graduating from high school and only 20 percent had even been in a bookstore!

Fortunately, even if these figures were true then, they are certainly not true now. With the rise of the book chains such as Walden and B. Dalton, books and bookstores are far more numerous, accessible, and inviting now than they have ever been.

While publishers have occasionally decried the rise of the chains, claiming they exert too much influence on what is published, this rise has been the single biggest factor in expanding the bookstore audience for your book, *regardless* of your subject.

In the absence of accurate survey information on American book-buying habits, your best bet, once again, is your local bookstore. You can assume that the space given over by the store to a particular subject is a reasonably accurate measurement of the book-buying activity on that subject.

Don't just analyze the general sections, but make note of the percentage of those sections devoted to a particular treatment or focus. In the "Baby and Child Care" section, for instance, what percentage of space is devoted to medical advice (Dr. Spock–type books), consumer advice, activity books, or pregnancy books, names-for-baby books, etc.

Are They Interested to the Tune of $15? Fifteen dollars is about the minimum a hardcover book costs these days. Yet for many people that is still a hefty sum.

Can you think of any way to shape or focus your idea that would make it *worth* that much? In fact, don't overlook the most obvious question of all: would *you* pay $15 for your book?

As a final thought on knowing your readers, I'm reminded of a comment once made to me by the writer and film critic, Richard Schickel. Schickel has also produced and directed programs for both network and public television, and though the networks obviously pay better, he prefers working within the intimacy of PBS. "Public television," he said, "delivers an *audience*, while the networks deliver a crowd."

I think it is helpful to perceive your readers in much the same way—as a small, intimate audience, even if that audience potentially numbers in the millions. Your reader-ship is linked by a shared interest and a common passion—your book. And whether your job is to make them laugh, hold them spellbound, or simply to inform them, if you are on intimate terms with your audience, you are far more likely to know how to turn them on.

KNOWING YOUR COMPETITION

Just as the subject of your book or manuscript will require some research, so does your book idea. Publishers will be judging your submission not only in terms of your demon-strated mastery of the subject and its intrinsic salability but also in terms of the competition. You need to know what else is out there, the books which have been recently published on the same or a related subject, and the slant and focus these books have taken.

If your idea is particularly hot or timely, or follows in the wake of several successful books on a particular subject, you can assume that the publishing house has already received dozens of proposals along similar lines.

This should not be an excuse to abandon your project or even to get discouraged. Publishers are constantly on the lookout for a new twist or slant on a popular theme. But in order to explain how your idea is a quantum leap forward, you will need to demonstrate a thorough working knowledge of your competition.

Even more important, knowing your competition helps you to focus your own thoughts and ideas and to choose your best approach. You may find that almost the exact same book you have in mind has already been published, in which case you may need to cut your losses. But what will often happen is that in contemplating the competition, and how to get around it, you will come up with an even better approach.

Most aspiring writers are aware of the importance of knowing their competition, but they fallaciously assume this information can be solely determined from the inventory of their local bookstore or from a trip or two to the library.

For the purpose of scouting your competition, libraries aren't much help at all. Considering the short anonymous life span of most books, a large percentage of the titles on a library's shelves are dated or no longer in print, thus making it difficult to draw an accurate picture of the recent or current publishing activity in a particular subject area.

And while bookstores can be a reliable measurement of what has been recently published (checking out the competition is a legitimate goal of your investigative trips to the bookstore) the constant avalanche of new titles turns even the balanced, well-stocked stores into, at best, a representative sampling of what is actually out there.

Keeping up with bestseller lists or subscribing to *Publishers Weekly* (page 71) can help, but in order to assure that you are thoroughly familiar with your terrain, you are going to have to turn to *Books in Print.*

Books in Print. *Books in Print* is an alphabetical listing of all books that are currently in print. It is updated annually in October (supplements are published bimonthly), and it is published in six volumes, two each (A–M and N–Z) under author, title, and subject. You are interested in the two volumes that are alphabetized by subject headings, appropriately called *The Subject Guide to Books in Print.*

The *Subject Guide* contains the titles, authors, and publishers of approximately 600,000 in-print books. To use it, simply look up your subject, idea, or key words from your title under the appropriate headings. Under many headings related headings are also suggested.

Almost all bookstores and libraries use *Books in Print* for their own reference, and they are usually happy to make it available to their customers upon request.

The first and most important point that can be made about *Books in Print* is: *do not let it discourage you.* Upon first turning to it, the extensive listings under almost any major subject will be enough to have you thinking about abandoning not only your idea, but the very notion of ever getting published.

Fortunately, most of the titles listed in *Books in Print* should not concern you. Remember, it contains all books in print: academic treatises and scholarly works; technical publications; books with tiny printings; back list books that remain in print but just barely; even privately published works where the author has taken the trouble to copyright the book and to inform the R.R. Bowker Company (*Books in Prints*'s publisher).

As a general rule, confine your research and concerns to those titles published within the last five years, and give far more weight and consideration to those titles published under familiar, recognizable imprints. This should immediately eliminate one-half to two-thirds of the titles listed under most headings.

However, even with these guidelines, the number of listings under many headings can still be daunting. That brings up the second most important point to be made about *Books in Print: do not take these listings literally.*

Your purpose in turning to *Books in Print*, in addition to sizing up your competition, is to size up your market— to sharpen your own sense of your book's audience as a function of what has already been published for it. As with bestseller lists, you are looking to "read between the lines," to extrapolate information rather than simply extract it.

Do the number of recent books under brand name imprints indicate a glut or dearth of published information in the marketplace? What direction and points-of-view do most of these titles take? How many other titles take your particular slant or focus? What underlying messages do these titles reveal about their audience? Are there any obvious or overlooked opportunities? These are the kinds of questions you should bring to *Books in Print*.

Recently, for instance, we were investigating the idea for a book on how to care for aging parents. In turning to the appropriate subject headings (Aging, Parents, etc.), we discovered a good many titles had already been published in this area. Most, however, were straightforward informational books which took a dispassionate approach. This knowledge led us to refocus our own thoughts on the subject. By taking a more qualitative, compassionate approach (*Loving Care for an Aging Parent*) we were able to give our book a unique identity and set it apart from much of the competition.

Later on, *Books in Print* will be a valuable reference source in researching and writing your book. But for now, if used correctly, it will help you see the big picture, and where, within the big picture, the opportunities lie.

KNOWING THE REALITIES

One of the most important by-products of thoroughly thinking your idea through is that you begin to get some sense of what it will take to make it real, of the time and work the manuscript will ultimately require.

Just as it is naive to believe that all that separates you from collaborating with Henry Kissinger is a phone call, it is foolish to pursue an idea that will eventually demand only slightly less time and effort than it took to build the Pyramid of Cheops.

Surprisingly, many aspiring authors fail to take into account the difficulty of executing their own ideas. They get so caught up in their own expansive enthusiasms they finesse the time-and-motion considerations or ignore them altogether.

I once saw a proposal for a book, which, if executed properly, would have required the author to interview about five hundred people (not a questionnaire, which would have been difficult enough, but face-to-face interviews). That would have taken three years even before the first word was written.

I know of another proposal, which was actually bought by a publisher for an advance of $20,000, which required its two authors to travel over 200,000 miles in order to deliver the manuscript.

I also once met with a woman who had compiled and written a 700-page almanac, *single-handedly.* (Almanac publishers hire a staff of twenty for much the same job.) Her almanac had sold modestly well—almost 20,000 copies—and we were discussing new projects she was interested in pursuing. But I wasn't concentrating. All I kept thinking about was that this woman had spent the last three years of her life working for fifty cents an hour.

At the other end of the spectrum is *The One Minute Manager.* With its ensuing success, this 10,000-word opus has earned its authors about $300 a word. That, along with *Jonathan Livingston Seagull* and Kahlil Gibran's *The Prophet,* has to rank near the top of any all-time time-and-motion bestseller list. (My own efficiency winner was *The First Family Paperdoll and Cutout Book.* It was thirty-two pages long and, being a cutout book, sixteen of the pages were blank.)

It would be misleading to talk about time and motion without making some reference to those books which are literature, art, or labors of love, those works which are so fueled by the author's passion for his or her subject that time and income become insignificant. Most definitive biographies and of course much of the world's great literature would have to be considered labors of love. (Can one imagine Tolstoy being "pressed for time"? Interestingly, however, Shakespeare would be a major exception. Time and money were the driving forces in his work: he had a theater to fill. If he had not, his complete works might· have consisted of a few sonnets.)

From the publisher's perspective labors of love are not only commendable but essential. Indeed, the industry might not be able to survive without them.

Aspiring authors, however, should analyze their book ideas in the harsh light of reality. They must go in with their eyes open and consider any project they are about to pursue in terms of the time it will take and the work it will involve. If these are of little concern, that's fine, so long as that is a decision which is consciously made rather than the result of hazy, lazy thinking. Otherwise, it is remarkable how quickly a labor of love can turn into a labor of hate.

"Someone's Already Thought of It." One of the harsher realities that aspiring authors must face is discouragement. The more properly and thoroughly you investigate your own idea, the greater the chance of discovering that someone else has already beaten you to the punch.

With 600,000 books in print this is hardly a remote possibility. And though one of the main purposes of your investigation is to uncover precisely this sort of information (so as to refocus or counter-program your own idea or maybe to come up with an even better one), the mind can do funny things. Just as your intuition can lead you to a good idea, your psyche's defense mechanism is already looking around for a reason to abandon it. And a book on a related topic with a remotely similar slant is often all the ammunition it needs.

Even if your idea is a genuine state-of-the-art advancement over what else is out there, your mind will still be hoping to bail out. Usually the most available rationale is "If my idea is any good, I'm sure someone else has already thought of it."

This, of course, is the perfect no-win, self-defeating attitude (reminiscent of the classic Groucho Marx line: "I'd never join any club that would have me as a member").

In truth, if you do have a good idea someone probably has already thought of it. And if you're lucky it may be one of the editors to whom you will be submitting your proposal.

Remember the editor? The one that's too busy writing cover copy, returning phone calls, and attending sales conferences? Again, this is another case where publishing's awful realities work to your advantage. That editor probably has fifty ideas that he or she simply has not had the time to follow up. Suppose yours happens to be one of them.

But what about all those other people out there? If your idea is so great then surely hundreds of others have thought of it as well. Again, some of them probably have, and just like you, they are all probably in the process of talking themselves out of even giving it a shot. Fortunately for you, the herd rarely follows through on its own idea. And you can gain an enormous edge simply by *not* taking yourself out of the running.

CHAPTER 8
Tailoring Your Idea to a Book Market

With 53,000 new books chosen from perhaps a half-million new submissions each year, anything you can do to set your idea and your proposal apart can only work to your advantage.

To make your submission distinctive, you want to show an editor that you have considered your subject in its broadest terms, that you have analyzed the various approaches one might take to it, and that you have chosen your particular slant because it is the best one. And while a book proposal will most likely be your forum, even a well-written proposal cannot disguise a soft or mushy or poorly focused idea. An exceptional proposal always conveys an exceptional, distinctive idea.

EXPANDING, THEN FOCUSING A MARKET

Expanding and then focusing a market is the practical application of all you have learned about your reader and your competition. It is taking this information and factoring it into your idea.

Consider any possible way to expand your reader base—

your potential audience—without sacrificing interest.* A tennis book, for instance, might be expanded to cover all racquet sports. Yet you run the risk that in making the book more generalized, you vitiate the interest of your core tennis-playing audience.

On the other hand, if your idea appeals primarily to working women or new mothers, it is worth asking yourself if there would be any great sacrifice of interest by expanding it to include all working people (i.e. people with too much to do and not enough time to do it in) or all new parents, both mothers and fathers.

Once you have satisfied yourself on this score you must "narrow-focus" your market. This is the most crucial phase of the entire conceptual process.

Narrow-focusing your market is tapping in on the all-important connections between your book and the subliminal motivation of its buyers. What twist, slant, focus, can you give your idea, what common motivation can you tap, what "passion button" can you push, *so that the majority of your potential market believes that your concept is uniquely tailored to them?*

Let me give a progressive example of how this might work:

Several years ago, the publishing industry jumped on the home computer bandwagon with a glut of titles on how to use them. Most of these books took the form of "Understanding" or "Using" or "Mastering" this home computer or that one.

For us computer illiterates, this was a very intimidating period. Not only did we feel stupid because we didn't know how to operate them (especially when our six-year-olds did), but home computers also engendered "math anxiety"—that awful feeling of one's mind glazing over when confronted

*One caution: Think twice about multi-topic concepts, even if the topics are related, where you are asking the reader to buy an entire book for one applicable chapter. This is a flaw found in many weak-selling nutrition or fitness books: one chapter for joggers, one chapter for golfers, one chapter for swimmers, and so on.

with anything more mathematically complex than balancing a checkbook.

This was such a common feeling that it is unlikely that a concept embodied in the title *Understanding Your Crabapple Computer* would have sold very well, because most of us would have assumed, probably correctly, that we probably never could.

The *Crabapple Computer Made Simple* is a little better, but ironically, *The Crabapple Computer for Idiots* is even better than that, reassuringly implying that you aren't the only idiot out there.

But perhaps the best of all might have been *The Crabapple Computer for Math Dropouts*. Now *there* is a book victims of math anxiety can relate to. "That," the reader might say, "is a book for me."

Fortunately, for aspiring authors there are new anxieties and new problems to be solved arising all the time. Once tax reform is passed, for instance, I would not be surprised if *Simplifying Tax Simplification* (or a similar title conveying the same concern) quickly appears on some publisher's list.

In addition to new problems that will need solving, with nearly 600,000 titles out there, it is amazing how many old veins still have gold in them, how many traditional concepts are just waiting for someone to come along and give them a new twist.

Recently, for example, I was involved in the packaging of a book on houseplants. Though there are hundreds of titles already on the subject, the author perceived that the majority of houseplant owners do not share the horticulturist's passion for all things green. What this potential audience *really* wanted, he surmised, were houseplants that looked good, required little care and caressing, and wouldn't die in a week. The title he selected to convey this approach was *Seventeen Houseplants Even You Can't Kill.*

It should be emphasized that fine-tuning your idea and sharpening its focus does not mean that your market will be smaller. In fact, just the opposite: by finding and hitting that common chord, you may lose part of your potential market, but the remainder will be more "real" than ever.

There are even those rare books that not only hit a common chord, but a common chord that is nearly universal. Who, for instance, at some time in life, has not loved and lost and suffered through the terrible heartache that followed? The poet, Peter McWilliams, figured that one out, and the book he co-authored, *How to Survive the Loss of a Love*, has sold over 2.5 million copies.

There are no set formulae for correctly focusing a market. Moreover, for many books that get published (novels, for instance) it only indirectly applies.

But if you have correctly sized up your audience, and in getting to know your readers you have accurately perceived their needs and desires, take advantage of this information, not just in writing your book, but in shaping and focusing your idea.

ADDING VALUE

Book ideas can often be targeted to a market by adding the value of a desirable, salable element.

Several references have already been made to this—adding to a fitness book the desire to "get it over with," for instance (*Total Fitness in Thirty Minutes a Week*). But these additions do not necessarily have to be qualitative. It can also be people or places or things. Here are a couple of the more obvious ways in which this is often done:

Get Your Idea Accredited. Lend credence to your idea by lending it credentials. Get someone involved (minimally with a testimonial or book introduction, or even as a collaborator) whose title or degree will give it an authority, or a cachet, that you or your idea might not otherwise have.

Experts abound, and with a good idea, it is easy enough to find one who will work with you, provide guidance and expertise, and lend his or her name (and the letters that follow the name) to your project.

Consider also the unaccredited expert, or someone who can lend expertise or credibility to your concept by virtue of his or her background, experience, or profession. If, for instance, you consider yourself an expert on surviving tax audits, having done so for each of the last twenty years, and wish to share this knowledge with others, you are still better off convincing an ex-IRS agent to be your book collaborator. Readers will automatically assume that an ex-IRS agent knows more about the tricks of the audit trade than you ever could.

Add a Brand Name. Once a book hits the stands it shares similarities with cornflakes; a book attached to a recognized brand name is much more likely to attract attention than one that isn't.

"Brand names," as used here, can be companies, or people (celebrities or personalities or recognized experts), or even institutions.

You are going to have to pay for "brand identification," usually in terms of a percentage of the book's advance and royalties. There is also the problem of access. But do not automatically assume that brand names are unavailable to you.

Weight Watchers, for instance, does not need your help in writing its cookbooks. But suppose twenty years ago (before they had published their first cookbook), you had approached them with the idea of lending the Weight Watchers name to a cookbook.

Are there any national organizations, museums, clubs, institutions, church groups, even corporations where, as a member or participator, you may indeed have access?

Consider Public Domain. "PD," or Public Domain, is a term that both attracts and horrifies publishers. It is used to cover anything which properly belongs to the public, and which therefore cannot be protected by copyright or trade-mark. Books where the copyright has expired are within the public domain, as are generic terms ("aerobic," "breakdancing"), publicly owned institutions (The U.S. Navy, The White House) and information (anything published by the Government Printing Office), * and any common term or expression ("yuppies," "Uncle Sam," "Christmas").

Even titles, by themselves, cannot be protected by copy-right, though obviously characters and content are. If, for instance, you were doing a book on cyclones, you would be perfectly within your rights to call it *Gone with the Wind.*

Two examples of how one form of PD can be used to add value are the "Scarsdale" and "Beverly Hills" diet books. Almost any public place is free territory and fair game, and some, such as these two, are so loaded with meaning ("young, rich, beautiful—and *thin*—people live there") that grafting them onto your idea can give an otherwise soft concept a very strong focus and handle.

What is and what is not public domain is often a tricky question, and one which is therefore better left to the lawyers than to this book. It is, however, an option, a way of adding value, that is worth exploring if and when a natural fit occurs.

Several years ago, for example, we packaged a book of edited and rewritten survival information from the Navy, Army, and Air Force which was provided to us by the Government Printing Office. As yet another generic survival book it probably would not have even been published, but titled *The U.S. Armed Forces Survival Manual* it has sold extraordinarily well in the United States and has been translated into seven foreign languages.

---

*The Government Printing Office is a goldmine of dry, dull public domain publications waiting to be given a creative slant or twist. For their catalogue or more information write to: Assistant Public Printer, Superintendent of Documents, Government Printing Office, Washington, D.C. 20402. Or call: 202-783-3283.

YOUR TITLE

The odds on your proposal's title actually ending up on your book are less than 50/50. There are any number of reasons for this, ranging from the publisher's desire to have its say to the often correct assumption that the best title will be suggested by or emerge from work on the manuscript.

Many books are indeed contracted for under the "title" "Untitled Novel" and "Untitled Non-Fiction." This usually occurs when there is a publisher/author consensus that the best title has yet to turn up, or when a publisher acquires a new work by an author they have already published.

The title on *your* submission, however, becomes much more important. In fact, for reasons that can be easily explained, your title may be *the single most important selling tool you have at your disposal.*

From the moment your submission enters the publishing house, it runs the constant risk of being grouped with all the other unsolicited submissions—i.e. awarded a kind of self-fulfilling amateur status. A great title is your best opportunity to quickly communicate the essence of your idea, and a title that jumps off the page immediately makes your proposal an editor's business. All of a sudden it becomes a find. Miraculously, your proposal is transformed from just another piece of straw into the golden needle in the haystack.

Moreover, once a great title comes into a house a publisher doesn't want to let go. The editor will *want* to work with you to further develop your concept until it lives up to your title. (I know of several instances where a book has been contracted for on the strength of a great title alone.)

It should be pointed out that if you are submitting fiction, your title, good or bad, will be less of a factor in the publisher's decision-making process. However, a compelling title on any non-fiction submission will get you noticed faster than anything else you can say, write, or do.

The Elements of a Good Title. An exceptionally strong book title is more often the result of inspiration than analytical thought, thus making it inherently difficult to discuss. If, for instance, you were to ask a group of editors what goes into making a good book title, the answer would probably be, "I'm not sure, but I know one when I see one."

As a general rule, however, a good title should be both informative and provocative: it must tell you in no uncertain terms what the book is about, and it should do this in some memorable and tantalizing way. If the idea for the book itself is strong then the most tantalizing title may be a straightforward statement of its content (*How to Win Friends and Influence People* or the many *My Story* titles on autobiographies of famous people). Otherwise it must express the right thought that most compellingly links the book to its readers.

Strong titles are often the result of a collaborative creative effort—two people playing off each other until the right thought or phrase hits. Titles can even grow out of casual conversations, presuming, of course, the author is listening for it.

The writer and sports announcer Dick Schaap once told me that when he was collaborating with the all-Pro Green Bay Packers' lineman Jerry Kramer, they had almost finished their book before figuring out what to call it. One day, while they were viewing videotapes of that year's Superbowl, the cameras panned in from several angles to show Kramer's key block on the winning touchdown that earned him that year's MVP award. "Thank God for instant replay," Kramer joked.

"That's our title," Schaap said. *Instant Replay,* a retelling of the Packers' championship season, went on to become a bestselling sports classic.

In thinking about your title there are three common traps that you should avoid.

First, a title must stand alone, so don't depend on your subtitle to help you out. The subtitle can amplify, but it should *not* be used to complete your title's meaning. There is a very practical reason for this: subtitles are often left off of publishers' order forms, and if you can't tell a book by its title alone, neither can the bookstore owners.

Second, a good title will often link its readers at some subliminal level. So don't use your title to try and convince your readers of something they are not already subliminally prepared to believe, even if it may be true. For instance, a book entitled *Money Isn't Everything* is not going to sell, no matter how compelling your evidence might be.

Third, don't let the cleverness of your title overwhelm its meaning. This is a trap that ensnares publishers as often as it does authors. To give but one of many examples, many years ago an insightful book on the investment business was published under the title *Dance of the Money Bees*. You guessed it. It ended up on the "Nature" and "Hobby" shelves.

While there may be no hard and fast title rules, other than, perhaps, what to avoid, there are certain title elements that seem to work consistently when matched with the right book or concept. The following list of some of these elements is illustrated by those bestsellers where it can be argued that their titles contributed to their success.

A Strong Direct Promise. (What you see is what you get): *Life Extension; Dress for Success; Eat to Win; How to Flatten Your Stomach; Nothing Down; Winning Through Intimidation; Think and Grow Rich; How to Avoid Probate.*

A Softer Direct Promise. (What you see would be nice): *The Joy of Sex; The Magic of Thinking Big; The Power of Positive Thinking; Pulling Your Own Strings.*

The Use of You or Your. (Putting your reader into the title—"This is a book for me"): *You Can Profit from a*

Monetary Crisis; What They Don't Teach You at Harvard Business School; You Can Negotiate Anything; Everything You Always Wanted to Know About Sex. (Note: The "you" is understood in titles that begin with an action verb. For example, "You can" *Dress for Success;* "You can" *Eat to Win.*

Provocative. ("I want to know more"): *Megatrends; Passages; Future Shock; The Amityville Horror; The Hidden Persuaders; Inside the Third Reich; Is There Life After Death?*

Empathetic. (Author as group therapy leader): *I'm Okay, You're Okay; When Bad Things Happen to Good People; How to Be Your Own Best Friend; Games People Play.*

Clever Double Takes. (They stop you in your tracks): Erma Bombeck's titles (*The Grass Is Always Greener Over The Septic Tank,* etc.); *Your Erroneous Zones; Up the Organization; From Those Wonderful Folks Who Brought You Pearl Harbor.*

Discordant. (Oxymoronic titles also stop you in your tracks): *Body Language; The One Minute Manager; Calories Don't Count.*

Definitive. (The source): *The Complete Book of Running; Total Woman; The Best of Mary Ellen's Helpful Hints; The Whole Earth Catalogue.*

Syndromes, Principles, and Complexes. (Unwritten "laws," undiagnosed "diseases"): *The Peter Principle; Murphy's Law; The Cinderella Complex; The Relaxation Response; The Peter Pan Syndrome; The Impostor Phenomenon; The Culture of Narcissism.*

As the above listings indicate, many effective titles begin with "How," "What," or "When," these being efficient words for getting you directly into your title's meaning.

Again, however, there are no pat rules or "magic" words that will lead you to a great title. Your best clue lies in knowing your readers. For if your title succeeds in subliminally connecting your book to its audience, it is, by definition, a great one.

SECTION III

Beating Them at Their Own Game

CHAPTER 9
The Great American Book Proposal

I t wasn't always so, but today fully 75 percent of all books sold to trade publishers are acquired on the basis of a proposal. For non-fiction that figure may run as high as 90 percent.

While some editors lament having to judge a book on the strength of twenty-five to thirty pages, the industry on a whole has encouraged this trend. Things simply move too quickly and editors have little choice other than to spend their manuscript-reading time only with that fraction of submissions that they have already acquired. (It is not unheard of for an editor to ask the author of a completed manuscript to draw up and submit a proposal for it.)

In truth the editors would have little choice anyway, for as long as one house is willing to consider proposals, then to be competitive they all must.

The book proposal is therefore the basic forum for communication between you and the publisher. And unless it is well thought out, professionally presented, and compellingly written, it will probably be your last forum.

THE NON-FICTION PROPOSAL: GENERAL CONSIDERATIONS

A book proposal is a vessel created to hold 1) the results of your thinking about your book and its market (as discussed in the previous three chapters), and 2) a thorough description of the book's contents. Unless your proposal delivers on both accounts, it is simply not going to hold water.

Assuming that you do have the goods, a proposal becomes mostly a matter of form following function, with your function being to say as compellingly as you can whatever you can to convince a publisher to buy your book.

Pull Out All the Stops. Remember that it is *your* job to make it the editor's job to read your proposal, and right now that isn't part of his or her job description.

Don't hold back. Pull out all the stops. Assume that you will never have the opportunity to say to that editor "I should have added..." or "I should have emphasized..." or "What I meant to say was..."

But assume nothing else. Do *not* assume that the editor will draw a favorable parallel between your book and a similar one currently residing on the bestseller list. Point it out. Do *not* assume that the editor knows your book is unique. Demonstrate it.

If your dad has promised to purchase the first ten thousand copies—say it (probably in the first sentence!). If your book's demographics are exceptional—show it. If it helps your cause to quote *Newsweek*, Lee Iacocca, the Bible or "Dear Abby" —do it.

A Good Book Proposal Is a Good Sales Proposal. Jim Bouton, the former major league pitcher and author of the bestselling *Ball Four*, is also the creator of another bestseller: Big League Chew, a novelty gum product (shredded bubble gum in a pouch) which became the candy industry's number one product the year it was introduced.

Jim, who understands the value of a good sales proposal, is frequently asked to speak to high school and college creative writing classes. His reality message: while turning the well-turned phrase and rhyming the perfect couplet are nice, the real world turns on effectively written proposals. So for yourself, write poetry, but for others learn to write good proposals.

A good book proposal is a good sales proposal. It is less an example of writing style than it is a justification of why your book should be published.

You are the seller soliciting a potential buyer, so use your proposal to make a good sales pitch. A good book proposal, in fact, should have more in common with a good proposal for a new product than it does with literature.

Make the Best Use of the Facts Available to You. This, of course, is the salesman's bread and butter. Position your facts to present your book in its best possible light.

If you are writing a plant book with the world's greatest living horticulturist, stretch out his pedigree over two pages. If you have only a brown thumb, tell how you finally managed to make your tomatoes grow, and how much value this will be to other brown thumbers.

With a little thought, you can use almost any fact about your book or your market to your selling advantage.

Don't Show Them the Engine Diagram. Show them the interior, let them kick the tires, even show them the engine. But *don't* pull out the engine diagram.

The greatest threat to effective proposal writing is going off on a tangent. It is always a temptation because you do want to demonstrate to the editor that you have a thorough understanding and knowledge of your subject and your market. But informational overkill can raise suspicions, for it may seem you are protesting too much ("If this is so good, why does he have to be *so* convincing?"), or worse, it can kill interest altogether.

Usually, these tangents take one of two directions. Either the writer gets too technical—gets so hung up on one point he or she can't get off of it—or the writer "forgets" that this is a proposal, and begins to write the book itself.

Recently, I was reading what I thought to be a fairly good proposal until I got to the author's discussion of his book's competition—which may have been the all-time thorough analysis of the published matter on the subject ever assembled. It went on for fifteen pages, fully half the length of the proposal. If it didn't kill an editor with boredom, which it probably would have, it would have most certainly dampened his or her enthusiasm for *any* book on the author's subject.

The other temptation—to begin to actually write the book within the proposal—usually occurs in the outline or chapter summary section. Here, of course, is where you feel the strongest need to show that you really do have a book. One paragraph leads to another and pretty soon . . . *Voila!* You have completed most of the first chapter, right there between your market analysis and your summary of Chapter Two.

This is so easy to do, but just as easy to correct. Simply be very self-critical in reading over your proposal, paying particular attention to information that may be fascinating to you and your ultimate reader, but of only passing interest to the middleman editor.

If any of your chapter summaries goes on for more than two or three pages, or if any one is conspicuously longer than all the others, then you may have started to write your book.

A Good Chapter Summary Suggests the Book Is Already Written. There will be more later on about the all-important

"Chapter Summary" section of your proposal, but it is worth pointing out here that just as there is often a temptation to begin to "write your book" in your chapter summary there is also a temptation to try to write your chapter summaries before you are even sure you have a book.

An effective chapter summary will not only convince an editor that you have a book worth publishing but that a great deal of time and thought has gone into its suggested organization. This, in turn, will give the editor confidence in your mastery of your subject and in your ability to execute your own idea.

The catch, however, is that you can't fake it. You can't write an effective chapter summary until you have put in the necessary time thinking about your book and how to best organize it.

In those sections of your proposal where you describe your market or your book's salability there is room to round off a few corners, to stretch the facts a bit or at least to present them in their best possible light.

But you can't bluff (with any consistent success) the outline portion of your proposal. If it is too skimpy, it raises skepticism; if it is poorly organized it raises concern; if it is mostly garbage, it raises suspicion.

The bottom line is that your chapter summary must read as though your manuscript has already been written and that *you are merely summarizing it for the editor's convenience.* Until you can do this, the rest of your proposal will be just so much hot air.

Knowing that you have to present your summary in this manner should force you to do much of your organizational thinking (and thinking about the book itself) at the time when it is most appropriate, which is before your proposal is written and submitted, rather than after it has been turned down. If it is any consolation, once your book is under contract, it will be much easier to write if you are working from a detailed, thoroughly thought out, and well-organized outline.

THE NON-FICTION PROPOSAL: SPECIFIC CONSIDERATIONS

There is no standard format for a book proposal. On several occasions, for instance, where a client has written a magazine piece which will serve as a basis of a book, I will submit the piece itself along with a covering letter from the author telling how he or she plans to go about expanding the piece into a book-length work (and why the effort is justified).

On other occasions, where I have been concerned that the formality of a book proposal might in some way stifle the client's natural passion for a subject or vitiate the strength of the idea, I have suggested that the author write a letter to me that's personal yet suitable for forwarding to the editor, describing how the idea came to be and why it should be a book.

Though form may differ substantially from one proposal to the next, there are certain proposal basics, some based on conventions, some based on common sense, that most well-written proposals have in common.

A Book Proposal's Four Minimum Requirements. A non-fiction book proposal, in any form, must fulfill four minimum requirements:

1) It must define the book's audience. For first-time authors, who are not going to be given many benefits of the doubt, this should be both a quantitative and qualitative (passion factor, bookbuyers, etc.—see Chapter Seven) definition.
2) It must describe the book, both generally, in one or two paragraphs, and specifically, in your chapter summary.
3) It must show how your book fills a need of its audience. The stronger the connection you can make between (1) and (2), the greater your chances are of having your proposal favorably received.

4) It must show why you are qualified to write the book. Most of your "qualifications" will show up in the outline portion of the proposal, in that the better your grasp of your material the more convincing you are going to be. But don't be afraid to toot your own horn as well. Use any fact at your disposal that would further convince an editor that you are ideally, even uniquely, qualified to write your proposed book.

Sell the Sizzle Up Front and the Steak Near the Back. As is probably already apparent, a book proposal works out to be about half sales and half book description. It is generally best to do your selling up front (who your audience is and why they are going to buy your book) and then put the meat on the bone later on.

All else being equal, arrange your proposal in diminishing order of salability. In other words, lead off with your most compelling facts and proceed from there.

If, for instance, your audience is passionate, large, and easily reached through bookstores, that information should come somewhere near the front. If, on the other hand, you (or the person with whom you are collaborating) are uniquely qualified, or are privy to some extraordinary cache of information, or have some exceptional access to something or someone, you would do well to let the editor know about this as soon as possible.

Know Your Reader, the Editor. Your book may appeal to a broad readership, but your proposal is calculated to appeal to only one reader—the editor.

It might be helpful to think of your proposal in terms of the progressive response, as the editor reads along, that you want it to provoke. Ideally that response would go something like this: "Interesting"; "Not bad"; "This may be a book"; "This is going to be a big book"; "I hope no one else has seen this proposal."

Don't Go for "Style." Your proposal is being judged almost solely on its content. Your best stylistic "approach," therefore, is one that is clear, simple, and easy to read.

THE PARTS OF A PROPOSAL

Though book proposals can vary wildly in form, well-written proposals contain certain common elements or "parts" (often presented under their own headings), arranged in approximately the same order. And no matter what form your own proposal might take, you are invariably going to have to address the importance of those opening paragraphs.

Getting Started. Many writers find that the most difficult part of writing a proposal is getting started—writing those first two or three opening paragraphs. This is hardly surprising in that most writers are already aware that these opening paragraphs need to be a grabber.

Most editors read at only two speeds: slow, when editing a manuscript; and scan, when reading anything else. The editor, therefore, is liable to make a snap judgment on the strength of your first few paragraphs *or even your first sentence.*

Therefore, if you decide to wait until page four to make your Big Statement, and if the editor never happens to get that far, it is not the editor's fault, but your own.

The opening of your proposal is aimed at achieving one purpose and one purpose only: to catch the editor's eye—to get him or her reading and to keep him or her reading. I usually recommend one of two approaches:

1) Hit Them Over the Head First. An effective opening to a proposal is reminiscent of the old joke about the man and his mule. This mule, the man told his friend, always obeyed every command.

But when the man yelled "Gideyup," the mule just stood there—until the man hit the animal on the nose with a two-by-four.

As the mule started to walk the man's friend said, "Why'd you do that? I thought you said he obeyed every command."

"He always does," the man answered. "But first you have to get his attention."

Getting an editor's attention can be anything from an inviting or provocative first line, to one or two paragraphs in which you relate the best possible story, anecdote, or sales point that your book has to offer.

When Jackie Sorensen, who created the aerobic dancing movement, wrote her first book, aerobic dancing was still a relatively unknown phenomenon. She therefore began her book proposal with the following sentence: "Aerobic Dancing is a complete physical fitness program that whispers exercise and shouts fun."

Astronaut Pete Conrad's book proposal began: "I did not sleep very well the night before I went to the moon."

It would be very difficult for an editor to read those opening lines without wanting to know more.

2) Dig a Hole and Fill It. Use your first two or three paragraphs to define your market and to describe the gap (or gaps) which you believe exists in that market. Your succeeding paragraph should then show how your book fills that gap, or fills it better than any other book out there.

It may be helpful to think of these opening paragraphs as setting a scene or telling a small story, with a suggestion of your book idea serving as the climax.

To use an earlier example from Chapter Seven, one might indicate that while there are a dozen baby and child care guides serving twenty million new parents, all are lengthy, complete, definitive works. But when an emergency occurs a parent has neither the time nor analytical detachment to refer calmly to an encyclopedic work. One could argue, therefore, that a short, accessible book that treats only baby emergencies might find its niche in this marketplace.

There is no set formula for effective proposal openings. One of the best proposals I have ever seen, for instance, began with its author recounting "in story form" the time and place and unusual circumstances under which his book idea had occurred to him.

There is, however, a set purpose—to get the editor reading—and a set warning: do it quickly. If you are on page four of your proposal and are still working on your boffo opening, then go back and start cutting it, or choose a wholly different, more succinct introductory approach.

Get to the Point. For many writers, the second greatest problem, next to getting into the proposal, is getting on with it, or making a smooth and efficient transition from the introduction to all that is to follow.

The quickest and best way to get to the heart of your proposal and to leave your opening behind is to write: "I propose, therefore, a book on _____" or "I propose to write a book entitled _____." This one sentence, followed by one or two explanatory thoughts describing your concept, will take you where you want to go.

The Hook. The "one or two explanatory thoughts" just mentioned may be the most important sentences in your proposal.

It has been estimated that a book salesman has an average of thirty seconds to present a new title to a bookstore. Publishers are therefore forced to think in terms of a "hook" or "handle" or the one key statement about a book which distinguishes it from the other 53,000 new titles out there. Generally this hook is echoed throughout the promotion of the book, from catalogue copy, to jacket or cover copy, to the advertising headline.

If your key thought—your hook or handle—is in fact your title, then all the better. If it is not, then should you be able to describe your book, particularly the distinguishing features that set it apart "in twenty-five words or less." This is where, in your proposal, this description should come.

The Other Stuff. The other parts of your proposal (other than your opening and your chapter summary) are where you take the opportunity to further define your audience, your book, and the connections that exist between them. If you have structured your opening correctly, you have probably used facts, made assumptions, or drawn conclusions that require further proof, justification, or clarification. The pages that follow your opening should be used to *amplify* those opening themes, thoughts, and assumptions. (Your opening was your calling card; now you're going to show them what you're really up to.)

This amplification can be presented as a straight narrative or in narrative chunks under appropriate headings. In either case, it must anticipate and answer an editor's most obvious questions (and even questions that may not occur to the editor, but where your answer to them would score points for the home team).

THE MARKET — The description of your market can be anywhere from half a page to two to three pages. While it is advisable to quantify your market, your main purpose is to distill its essence as it specifically relates to the theme and slant of your book.

THE COMPETITION — This can be handled as a footnote paragraph to the market or under a separate heading, depending on which better serves your purpose.

And your purpose is this: to define the competition in terms of how it is *not* totally serving the needs of its audience, highlighting the gap that still exists which your book just happens to fill.

Also remember that you are known by the company you keep. When appropriate, make comparative references to bestsellers, while indicating how your book is slightly different or better.

THE AUTHOR — A writer's bio usually follows the chapter summary. However, the more impressive your credentials (or your background or expertise as it relates to your subject) the closer to the beginning of your proposal you will want this information to appear.

The author's bio should never be more than half a page, unless it is so intwined with the idea itself or so instrumental to the book's salability that a more considered recitation would outweigh the advantages of brevity.

Write your bio in the third person. An easy, efficient way to begin is "(YOUR NAME) is . . .".

THE BOOK — Most book proposals end up describing the author's book three times, with each description amplifying the one that has preceded it.

The first is the "one liner" hook or handle, which appears early on, either in the process of "filling in your hole" or in making your transition ("Get to the Point"). The third and final is the chapter summary itself. And the second and middle is "The Book," a one-half or two-page summary of the book's overall theme, organization, structure, and important elements, which usually immediately precedes the "Chapter Summary."

DELIVERY — This is usually the final heading of your proposal, and should not run more than one or two lines. It provides the publisher with two pieces of information: the estimated length of your manuscript, and the estimated time it will take you to deliver it.

The estimated length of your book should be given in the number of words and not in the number of pages. On average, a 200-page book would run around 75,000 words. However, if you are vague in your own mind about your book's projected length, find a book that "feels" like the book you intend to deliver, count the number of words on an average page, and multiply this by the number of pages in the prototype book.

The average time of delivery for most books (assuming you have yet to begin work on the manuscript) is eight to twelve months.

Other Headings. Since proposal form follows function there are any number of other headings you may wish to incorporate into your proposal. On occasion, for instance, where you can make a strong connection or several connections between audience and book, you might consider building your argument under a separate heading called "Rationale."

On other occasions, particularly when the idea for a book may be going against conventional perceptions, you might find it helpful to define the idea in terms of "What This Book Is Not."

The overriding dictum is: use your common sense. If, for instance, your book proposal raises any concern about your ability to gain certain access in order to execute your idea, you might want to consider a separate discussion under "Execution," "Methodology," or "Modus Operandi." If the book is exceptionally complex or has an important overriding structural or thematic principle, a section on "Structure" or "Organization" might be in order. If it is a book that requires subjective judgments as to what should and should not be included, state what those judgments are under a section labeled "Criteria for Inclusion" or "Method of Selection."

In other words, include any "parts" of a proposal that best serve your purposes and leave out any that don't. While you can't coerce or cajole an editor into buying your book, you can make a plausible argument to an editor as to why he or she should. Your forum for this is your book proposal, and this forum—how and what you choose to say—is totally within your control.

Your Chapter Summary. This is the core of your proposal, often half or more of its entire length, and containing all the main criteria on which your proposal will be judged.

These criteria—organization, thought, mastery of your subject, etc.—have already been emphasized. What remains to be discussed here are the two basic forms in which these summaries are usually presented.

If your book is strictly or primarily informational, short descriptive sentences or even sentence fragments will serve your purpose. Here, for instance, is a summary of one chapter from the proposal for the previously mentioned *U.S. Armed Forces Survival Manual:*

> CHAPTER IV: On the Move
>
> Route Selection — Following a Ridge — Following a Stream — Following Coast or Shorelines — Through Dense Vegetation — Travel Through Mountains — Snowfield and Glacier Travel — Crossing Water — Signalling While Traveling — International Ground-to-Air Emergency Code.

What this form gains in efficiency it loses in terms of excitement; therefore the preferred form is short (anywhere from two paragraphs to two pages) narrative summaries of each chapter.

In some ways, these summaries are miniversions of the proposal itself. Ideally each should start with a specific thought (hook), story, or anecdote taken from the chapter (thereby indicating that you've got the goods), followed by one or two amplifying paragraphs on the general theme of the chapter or the territory it will cover.

From there, finish off the chapter summary quickly and efficiently. This can be done with one or two headings; bulleted subjects (begin with an ellipsis or bullet) the chapter will cover; questions the chapter will answer; or other devices of this sort. In other words, once you have given a

specific example and stated the chapter's parameters, summarize remaining pertinent thoughts before you move on to
the next chapter.

Here is a serviceable example of a narrative chapter
summary taken from a book proposal on job hunting:

> The Résumé: An Advertisement for Yourself.
>
> It is the most important piece of paper in your
> job search, and most people have trouble putting
> it together. We will do more than simply discuss
> the "perfect résumé." There will be a workbook
> section—space provided to write out a résumé as
> you go along. Also, rules, tips, do's and don'ts, along
> with examples of good résumés and lousy ones.
> Some of the points brought out in this chapter:
>
> — Résumés are not usually read; they're scanned.
>   (We will show what the résumé scanner looks
>   for, such as continuity of employment.)
> — What to avoid: the use of "I," historical
>   narrative, etc.
> — The use of action verbs. (We will supply a list
>   of 60.)
> — How to succeed without really lying: How to
>   make summer jobs and part-time work sound
>   important.
> — How to handle gaps in your employment record.
> — The acid test. Read over your completed résumé:
>   Would you hire this person?

There are two final points that should be made about the
chapter summary section of your proposal.

First, your idea may defy a detailed chapter breakdown, or
may fall into an area where such an exercise (an investigative
book, for instance) would look foolishly premature. If you
are certain this is the case (if you are not certain and end up
being wrong the absence of a detailed summary will work

against you), consider outlining or summarizing the book's larger divisions (its three or four sections or parts) or do an "outline of intent," explaining what you intend to find and how you intend to handle this information once you find it.

Second, your chapter summary is not carved in stone. A publisher does not expect you to follow your outline word for word, thought for thought. In fact, the publisher expects— would even encourage—quite the opposite. For once you get into research and writing the book itself, better organizational approaches, either to individual chapters or to the overall structure, will probably occur to you, or additional information will surface which will need to be handled and incorporated in some way.

This indeed, is why a detailed chapter summary is so important. Not only is it your most convincing selling tool, it is the organizational "base line" for the book itself, against which better, and eventually the best, stylistic, structural, and organizational approach can be measured.

THE FICTION PROPOSAL

The fiction proposal is an altogether different kettle of fish, and one with an immediate scent. For while a non-fiction proposal can be up to 50 percent sizzle, a fiction proposal is almost entirely steak.

The editor has little inclination and less time to develop fiction, to nurture unpublished talent (a published novelist has an obvious advantage), or to turn promise into fulfilled promise. With rare exceptions, a near miss is as good as a mile, and as far as the editor is concerned either you can write fiction or you can't.

The standard fiction submission (much more standard, by the way, than non-fiction) is, therefore, a ten- to twenty-page plot summary and two sample chapters. Any additional information, such as genre and author's background, is best handled in a covering letter.

Your work will be judged against the usual roundup of fiction criteria, but the overriding question an editor will be asking is *can you tell a story?* If you can't, your ability to create mood, character, atmosphere, etc. will almost certainly get you, at best, a reluctant rejection.

If your storytelling ability and the writing in your chapters appeals to the editor, you will receive a request to see more. Therefore, work as much of a strong story line as you can into the first two chapters.

TWO TECHNICALITIES

Last are the two questions about proposals that are most frequently asked, and therefore should be answered before moving on, even though both deal more with form than substance.

How Long Should a Proposal Be? As may have become obvious, a proposal should be as long as it has to be and not a word longer. Use every fact and argument available to you; position them correctly, say them succinctly, and don't digress or go off on tangents. Most proposals run around twenty to twenty-five pages in length.

What Is the Format? Your proposal should be neatly typed in black ink on 8½" x 11" white bond paper, and free of misspellings and typos. Lines should be double-spaced, triple-spaced around headings, and generous margins should be provided. While a form submission letter is disastrous, a photo-copy of the proposal itself is fine, even preferred. (Publishers don't want the responsibility of handling originals.)

As a final thought on book proposals, a smudged three-page proposal filled with misspellings obviously works against you. But keep in mind that a publisher would sooner make an offer for a sensational idea scrawled on a napkin than on a beautifully typed twenty-five-page proposal that says nothing.

CHAPTER 10
A Submission Strategy That Works

I f this were a novel, we would have now come to the payoff—or the submission process itself.

For those of you who have felt compelled to skip ahead ("to see how it comes out") or have turned directly to this chapter, I feel equally compelled to offer a caveat.

There is a submission strategy that should get you a response, and you can pick it up from this chapter alone. It is based on commonsense guidelines, drawn from what has already been written about an editor's "mental state," and the way the publishing industry operates. The catch is that these guidelines won't make much common sense to you if you haven't read some of what has already been discussed.

The main point, however, is that if you get a response from an editor, then your submission strategy has worked and you have won the battle. But if that response is the same as it would have been in a form rejection then you have lost the war.

The key to an effective submission strategy is to get yourself out of the slush pile and onto an editor's desk. But the overall purpose—the end rather than the means—is to get a positive response. Since much of this book has concentrated on achieving this end, this final chapter will focus on the submission process itself, which, even when successful, is still just the means.

THREE DON'TS

A discussion of submission strategy must begin with how not to begin, or what not to do at the outset in order to avoid losing the battle before it has even begun.

1) Do Not Send Your Manuscript As a First Salvo. If your first contact with an editor is your manuscript, then you are playing your game and not his and you will come out the loser. Even if your covering letter intrigues the editor, there isn't enough time in the day to deal with your manuscript. So it lies there, and lying manuscripts, like fish and house guests, begin to stink after a few days.

Moreover, the bigger initial package an editor has to deal with, the more raw material you are giving him or her on which to form the basis of a rejection.

2) Do Not Send a Self-Addressed, Stamped Envelope. This is no big deal, but I have always felt that a S.A.S.E. kind of begs rejection and becomes almost self-fulfilling. It also marks its sender as something of an amateur (can you imagine Norman Mailer enclosing one?) and as the reader of too many articles on how to get published.

3) Do Not Send a Form Letter. Form letters are considered bad form in most business situations; as a publishing submission it is suicidal. A form submission letter will, at best, get you a form rejection letter.

Form letters scream multiple submission, and while editors do not object to multiple submissions per se, if your proposal is on the fence, an editor who might have otherwise gotten back to you will assume someone else will and will simply file your proposal in his or her wastebasket.

TWO DO'S

1) Do address the editor by name. Submission letters addressed to "The Editor," "The Editorial Department," "Gentlemen," or "Dear Sir" are guaranteed grist for the slush pile mill.

Make sure the editor to whom you are sending your submission is a real live editor working at a real live publishing house. Once you have confirmed that the editor is, in fact, at that house (editors move around a lot), send your submission directly to that editor addressed to him or her *by name.* This alone should get you out of the slush pile and guarantee you a personal response.

This—addressing your submission to an editor *by name*—is the one absolute must in any submission strategy. When I mentioned to an editor at Doubleday that I thought that this one piece of advice would raise the response rate to unsolicited submissions by 50 percent, he was surprised.

"Fifty percent?" the editor said. "Eighty percent is more like it."

2) Do demand a response. Do not frame your submission inquiry in such a way that the editor can reject it by silence or by simply not responding ("If you are interested...").

Instead, end all inquiries by specifically asking for a response ("Thanks for considering my work. I look forward to hearing from you").

This forces an editor to take a look at your work (at the very least, to form a basis for rejecting it) and to give you an answer.

THE RIGHT NAMES AT THE RIGHT HOUSES

A totally successful submission campaign is obviously one that ultimately leads to a publisher offering a book contract. That will be determined, of course, by the strength of your idea and the manner in which you have presented it. But first you have to give yourself a fighting chance and that depends almost entirely on where, and to whom, you send your submission.

How do you select the editor and publisher who are most likely to be favorably predisposed to your submission? You are going to have to use some judgment and that judgment is going to be based on what you have learned from two sources: your local bookstore and *The Literary Marketplace* (or *LMP*).

The LMP. *The Literary Marketplace,* published by R.R. Bowker (the same folks who bring you *Publishers Weekly* and *Books in Print*) is the industry's phone book. Every bookstore and library has a copy* and almost without exception they will be happy to let your refer to it. The *LMP* is almost a thousand pages long and simply thumbing through it will give you a good idea of the services and suppliers that publishing a book requires.

The section of the *LMP* that should primarily interest you, however, is section one: "U.S. Book Publishers." This section is about 150 pages long and lists the names, addresses, phone numbers, and key editors of approximately 1,500 publishers. Of this number approximately half are trade (general) book publishers (the rest being academic or technical), and of this number half will be too specialized for your book (atlases, encyclopedias, religious books, etc.).

Once you weigh the other factors (the number of titles a house publishes, for instance), the bottom line is that only about 100 to 150 publishers listed in the *LMP* are going to be right for your book. Your job, obviously, is to find at least some of them.

For your purposes the *LMP* should be used both literally

---

* If you want to order your own *LMP* write to R.R. Bowker, 205 East 42nd Street, New York, N.Y. 10017—but at $55 I would advise against it. *LMP* is updated annually, so you might ask your librarian or bookstore manager to give you the old copy once the new one arrives.

VANITY PRESSES

These are publishers that will accept and publish your work, but unlike legitimate publishers *you pay them* (anywhere from $6,000 to $7,000 and up) to publish your book, rather than the other way around.

The main thing to know about vanity presses is that they thrive by exploiting people's gullibility (and vanity). They promise success—even bestsellerdom—when the truth is, bookstores rarely carry anything from a vanity publisher. They are not an alternative any legitimate writer should consider.

The fact that vanity presses charge the authors to publish their work is a dead giveaway, but sometimes their come-ons are so persuasive, and their "terms" so well camouflaged, it is difficult to tell. If at all in doubt check out the publisher's listing in the *Literary Market Place*. The *LMP* endeavors to weed out the vanity presses and eliminate them from its listings.

and interpretatively. Literally, of course, it gives you the names and addresses of publishers and the actual names of the editors who work there. Interpretatively, you are looking for publishers who are going to be most receptive to your particular book.

How to Size Up a Publisher from the *LMP*. Since only about one out of every fifteen publishers in the *LMP* is right for your book, it is easier to look for the ones that are right than to go through the entire listing eliminating all of those that are wrong.

To do this start with the list of major publishers on pages 126–127 in this chapter. If the *LMP* thoroughly confuses you, limit your submission to the publishers included on this list. But if you are good at detective work, check out the listing of several of these publishers in the *LMP* and use their *LMP* profiles as a clue to finding others that might also be appropriate.

In sizing up a publisher in the *LMP* here are other clues that you should be looking for:

- The types of books published. This is generally found near the end of each listing, and is your major clue.
- Number of titles published. If the number of titles published the previous year is less than fifteen, that publisher is probably too small to be interested in your book.
- Date founded. Small publishers go in and out of business faster than restaurants, so eliminate any publishers who have been around less than three years.
- Imprints. The reasons for the many imprints under one publishing roof are as numerous as the imprints themselves. An editor, for instance, may be given his or her own imprint as a reward for success and loyalty. Or it may represent a co-publishing venture or some form of distribution deal. However, the two main reasons imprints are created are 1) to identify certain formats and 2) to define a particular genre within the house.

Do not, therefore, send your submission to the editor of a particular imprint unless you are sure that your submission is appropriate for that particular imprint.

If, for instance, you wish The Putnam Publishing Group to consider your hardcover book and you send your submission to the Perigee (one of Putnam's trade paperback imprints) editor, you have already given that editor a great reason to reject it. (Editors will often refer good proposals to the appropriate division or imprint within the house, but you cannot rely on that.)

How to Use the Bookstore. Use your local bookstore to confirm your *LMP* findings, particularly regarding formats

ESTABLISHED PUBLISHING HOUSES

This partial list of some of the more well established publishing houses will help you get started in making your submission selections. Remember, however, that most large houses publish under several imprints and where applicable, your submission should be addressed to the appropriate imprint.

Trade Hardcover Houses

Addison-Wesley
Arbor House
Atheneum
Beaufort Books
Crown Publishers
Dodd Mead & Co.
Doubleday & Co.
E. P. Dutton
Farrar, Straus & Giroux
Harcourt Brace
   Jovanovich
Harper & Row
Holt, Rhinehart &
   Winston
Houghton Mifflin
Alfred A. Knopf

J. B. Lippincott
Little Brown
McGraw-Hill
Macmillan Publishing
   Co.
William Morrow & Co.
W. W. Norton & Co.
G. P. Putnam's Sons
Random House
St. Martin's Press
Charles Scribner's Sons
Simon & Schuster
Summit Books
Stein & Day
Viking-Penguin

Mass Market Houses
(all also publish trade paperbacks)

Avon
Ballantine/Del Rey/
   Fawcett
Bantam
Berkley Publishing Group
Dell

New American Library
   (Signet)
Pocket Books
Warner Books
Zebra Books

Trade Paperback Houses

Andrews, McMeel & Parker
Dolphin (imprint of Doubleday)
Fireside (imprint of Simon & Schuster)
Owl (imprint of Holt, Rhinehart & Winston)
Penguin (imprint of Viking-Penguin)
Perennial Library (imprint of Harper & Row)
Perigee (imprint of The Putnam Publishing Group)
Quill (imprint of William Morrow)
Touchstone (imprint of Simon & Schuster)
Vintage (imprint of Random House)
Workman Publishing Co.

Reference Book Publishers

Arco Publishing
Barnes & Noble Books
Barrons Educational
   Series
Basic Books
Chilton Book Co.
Dover Publications

Facts on File
Hearst Books (subsidiary
   of William Morrow)
McGraw-Hill
Nelson-Hall
Rand McNally
Van Nostrand Rheinhold

Religious and Specialty Publishers

Abbeville Press (art and "coffee table" books)
Abingdon Press (religious)
Harry N. Abrams (art and photography, "coffee table" books)
Basil Blackwell (scholarly books)
Hammond (maps, travel, reference)
H. P. Books (cookbooks and how-to craft books)
Methuen (scholarly and general non-fiction)
Thomas Nelson (religious)
Rand-McNally (maps, travel, reference)
Fleming H. Revell (religious)
Routledge & Kegan Paul (scholarly)
Shocken Books (religious)
Sunset Books (cookbooks/how-to)
Universe Books (art and architecture)
The Zondervan Corp. (religious)

and imprints, or to suggest leads that you can follow up in the *LMP.*

If you find a book that "feels" similar to the book you want to write, that may be one of your best clues. Check to see who published it and look them up in the *LMP.* (If you can't find a listing, refer to the title page and see if that particular publisher or imprint is actually "A Division of . . ." and check under the larger listing.)

Once you have a fairly good idea of a publisher to whom you wish to submit, you may also want to ask the bookstore manager to let you see the most recent catalogue from that particular publisher. The publisher's catalogue will help you confirm your impressions about the nature and makeup of a particular list.

Confirmation. The literal information in the *LMP* is what is going to be most helpful to you. It gives you the names and addresses of publishers and the names of specific editors to whom you want to address your submission. But it also gives you one other piece of literal information: phone numbers.

I am surprised by how few unpublished authors call the publishers to whom they wish to submit, not to sell over the phone,* but to get additional information to confirm or discount what they think they have already learned.

When calling a publishing house to seek or confirm information *do not* identify yourself as an aspiring author or as someone who has something to submit because if you do everyone from the phone operator on up will treat you "that way." Simply say that you are "seeking some information," "confirming some information," or "doing some research," which, of course, you are.

---

*Remember the written word is publishing's selling medium. Your chances of convincing an editor over the phone to take a look at your submission are less than remote. And, of course, if you choose that route and lose, you have also lost a customer for the more effective submission strategy recommended in this chapter.

Before you submit, there is one essential reason for calling the publishing house, and two other pretty good ones:

1) Confirm that the editor is still there. Editors move around so much that 25 percent of the names in a current *LMP* are likely to be inaccurate.

   Ask for the editorial department and confirm with whomever answers the phone that so-and-so is still there. If so-and-so is no longer there ask for the name (and spelling) of the person who has taken his or her place.

2) Ask for a catalogue. I think it is a good idea to first look through the catalogue of any publisher to whom you are considering sending your proposal. Have the operator transfer you to the sales department and ask whoever answers the phone to send you "their most recent trade catalogue." (Many houses have a catalogue for each imprint, so if the response is "which one?" have your answer ready.) You may have to beg a little, but you will be surprised how many publishers will comply.

   Sales and publicity personnel, by the way, are not as hardened to the plight of the unpublished author as editors are and if you end up revealing why you want to see their catalogue they probably won't hold it against you.

3) Don't forget the "Stephen King trick" referred to in Chapter One. If you see a book that is similar to yours, look up the publisher, call the editorial department, and ask for the name of the editor of that particular book.

   Everyone appreciates anyone who has done his or her homework, and I can't think of a better way to begin a submission letter than to write: "As the editor of *Such and Such*, which I greatly admired, I thought you might be interested in considering my proposal for . . ."

SUBMISSION TACTICS

Once you know where you are going to send your submission, and to *whom*, it is quite natural to ask, "So what should I be submitting?"

The answer is . . . it depends. It depends on what you have to submit and the tactics or gamesmanship you feel will best work to your advantage.

First, obviously, observe the three Don'ts and the two Do's covered at the beginning of this chapter. Second, make sure your proposal is already written and ready to go even if, after reading on, you decide it should not be sent as your opening move.

From here on, other than fiction submissions, you are going to have to play it by ear. Fortunately you don't have to be Beethoven to pick up the key.

The Fiction Submission. Since the proof is totally in the pudding there is no use playing around. Write a brief covering letter which makes reference to your genre and perhaps conjures up a name or two of a bestselling author or book which has inspired or is similar to your own work. Your outline and your two sample chapters (as described in the previous chapter) should accompany this letter.

The Non-Fiction Submission. The non-fiction submission requires a little more thought, the thought being whether it is better to fire off your proposal or a letter of inquiry as your opening salvo.

The main disadvantage to a letter of inquiry is that you are two steps removed from a meaningful response. The letter of inquiry asks: "Would you consider my proposal?" and the proposal that follows says: "Here's what I am asking you to consider," thus making the question of considering and the act of considering two distinct steps.

Also, your proposal may so totally speak for itself that to summarize it in a letter of inquiry or to refer to it in any way other than "Enclosed please find . . ." shortchanges your idea and weakens your argument for publication.

If you believe this to be the case, then your proposal *must* speak for itself—i.e. your covering letter must be short, no more than half a page—and to the point. In addition to the title, it should contain *at most* a one- or two-line description of your book, perhaps a comment about the number of editors to whom you have sent it (more about that in a moment), and a closing remark about your desire for a timely response. *And that's it.*

Your covering letter would therefore look something like this:

Dear Mr. Von Braun:

    I am pleased to enclose for your consideration my proposal for a book entitled Green Cheese, which incorporates every known myth, fact, song, legend, and romance about the moon into a single volume.

    I have taken the liberty of sending this proposal to more than one house but naturally I would like nothing more than to be part of the Acme House list.

    I look forward to hearing from you at your earliest convenience.

                             Sincerely,

I believe, however, that the above approach should be the exception. Assuming that your proposal remotely lends itself to summary, I would recommend a letter of inquiry as your best first shot to take at a publisher.

The Letter of Inquiry. A letter of inquiry as your submission gambit makes sense for several reasons. First, it solves the problem of *time*, that one thing that no editor seems to have enough of. The evaluation of a one- to three-page submission letter is much quicker than of a twenty-five-page proposal, and is therefore easier to deal with.

Second, the editor has a much easier decision to make. You are simply asking the editor if he would like to *see* your proposal (which requires a simple "Yes, I would" or "No, I wouldn't" answer.). No publishing determination or consideration has been asked for and none is required. So the editor loses nothing in asking to see your proposal and loses something (maybe a book, maybe unsatiated curiosity) in saying no.

Third, a taste of honey is sometimes better than the whole jar. A good submission letter will whet the editor's appetite for the proposal to follow.

Finally, and most important, I believe a letter of inquiry "gets 'em a little bit pregnant." Once an editor asks to see your proposal that editor is on the hook whether he or she is aware of it or not. Implicit in asking you to send your proposal is an obligation. The editor now *owes* you a careful, considered response, maybe even a benefit or two of the doubt, and at least some specific editorial advice.

Additionally, you are now on a one-to-one basis with the editor. You have a correspondence going. While you may not be on a first name basis, at least you are no longer a total stranger or just another one of those unpublished authors trying to turn an editor's head.

What should a good letter of inquiry contain? It should be the best of your proposal, and, to a large extent, should parallel the opening or introduction of your proposal. Do not be reluctant to extract direct phrases or paragraphs from your proposal for your letter of inquiry. In fact, if your proposal is any good, you will probably want to.

Go easy on the chapter summary and use instead the hook or handle or transition description that appears early on in your proposal.

In addition, your letter of inquiry should briefly define

your audience and show how your proposed book fills a need of that audience. If your credits, experience, and background are salable you might want to throw a little bit of that in as well.

Just as you don't want to start writing your book in the middle of your proposal, you don't want to start writing your proposal in the middle of your letter of inquiry. Keep it short, one to three pages max.

Remember that your letter of inquiry has but one purpose: to leave the editor salivating for your proposal. Less is therefore more. In fact, the less said, other than your most tantalizing facts and your most delectable morsels, the better your letter of inquiry is going to be.

The Manuscript Problem. Suppose you have already completed your manuscript. When do you send it? This will sound odd, but I am going to recommend that you don't—not now, and not ever until it is time to deliver the final book.

When editors buy from a proposal—which is most of the time—they presume that the manuscript has yet to be written, which is true most of the time. I believe, therefore, that it is better not to disabuse them of this notion.

Better, I believe, to remove the manuscript from the submission process altogether and to submit a proposal for your book *even if it is already written.* In addition to giving the editor less to turn down, you will probably want to rework the manuscript anyway based on the editorial feedback you have received from the proposal.

If, however, your feeling is "this is my book, take it or leave it" (which is not the best attitude to have going in) and you insist upon having a publishing determination based on your manuscript, then your first written contact with the publisher should be a letter of inquiry which serves as a quasi-proposal. In other words, take your best shot. Write a longer than usual letter of inquiry which incorporates the functions of a proposal discussed in the previous chapter,

DEAD GIVEAWAYS

There are certain recurring phrases in submission letters that immediately reveal the amateur status of the sender:

- "This is a humorous book about..." (If your book truly *is* humorous let the editors discover this for themselves.)
- "My friends have read it and they all love it." (Unfortunately, publishers must feel the market is larger than your circle of friends.)
- "Perhaps my style is too literary, but..." (Meaning you find it difficult to write a simple declarative sentence or even *you* don't think it's a good story.)
- "A good idea for the cover would be..." ("...and while I'm at it, I also have a few tips for your sales department.")
- "This is your next bestseller." (The have-I-got-a-book-for-you approach does not work.)
- The redundant "This is a fictional novel..."

ending with "I have a completed manuscript, which I will be happy to send for your consideration."

How to Handle Multiple Submissions. Sending your submission letter or proposal to more than one publisher at a time, which I am going to recommend, raises an interesting question: do you inform the publisher of this piece of information?

On the one hand, if a literary agent or book packager multiply submitted a proposal and failed to inform the recipients, this would be considered bad form, and if done with any regularity, would result in a loss of credibility.

On the other hand, you have no credibility to lose, and as

an outsider you are not expected to know the conventions that dictate the multiple submissions process anyway.

Additionally, when an editor is part of a multiple submission from a literary agent, while the editor would have preferred to have an exclusive look, he or she will still definitely respond. If, however, *your* submission is anything close to borderline, and you have informed the editor that it is also a multiple one, you almost certainly will not be extended the same courtesy.

Even so, if you plan to make a multiple submission, I think you must reveal it to the recipient in some way. I would, however, suggest that you soft-sell it as much as possible.

You might want to emphasize, as I did previously in the sample covering letter, an implied preference for the house to which you are sending it. You may even want to plead ignorance or play on sympathies. ("Realizing that as an aspiring author my chances of getting published are very slim, I have taken the liberty of making several inquiries.")

However, the best solution may be to stagger your submissions, one per week. You can then write with total truth and equanimity: "I hope to hear from you at your earliest convenience, as there are other publishers to whom I would like to submit my proposal."

TEN GOOD NAMES

The reason for the above multiple submissions discussion is that I am going to suggest that the goal of all your earlier research and fact-checking is to end up with ten good names, meaning the names of ten live editors working for ten appropriate publishing companies, all of whom you have checked out.

There is nothing magic about the number ten; it could just as well be five or fifteen. But as long as it is more than two or three (too small to allow for "sampling error," i.e.

individual editorial opinion), your submission to this list should tell you all you need to know about the correctness of your submission strategy, the strength of your idea, and the effectiveness of your proposal.

If you get no response, or only one or two, or form rejections, then there is obviously something wrong with your submission strategy, or the people to whom you sent your letter or proposal aren't the ten good names you thought they were.

If you get six to ten responses and they are all negative, then there is something wrong with your idea or the way in which you have presented it.

Regrettably, if this occurs, it is more than just a failed market test. One of the great writer's myths is the one about papering walls with rejection slips. There are stories of proposals and manuscripts that were rejected twenty-five or thirty times and went on to become published books and even, in rare cases, bestsellers. But these stories are so exceptional that when they do happen they immediately become part of publishing lore.

Part of playing a publisher's game is knowing when you have lost. If you have been flatly rejected by ten well-chosen editors then you will almost certainly be turned down by the next hundred. It would be far better to spend your time rethinking your idea, reworking your proposal, or maybe even abandoning that particular idea and moving on to something else.

What you are hoping to receive is a request from one or two of the editors to see more material. Even better will be some suggestions or advice from these editors as to how to improve the quality of your work or how to make it more salable. If these suggestions are anything short of outrageous they should be incorporated into your proposal, at least in the revised version intended for the editor who made the suggestions.

In other words, be agreeable. An editor is far more likely to buy a book that he or she has helped shape.

If, as a result of submitting to your ten good names, you have one or more houses genuinely interested in making an offer it is time to get a literary agent.

PUBLISHING'S CATCH-22: THE LITERARY AGENT

Up to this point the literary agent has been conspicuously left out of the submission process (and indeed out of this entire book). This is because it is more difficult to get a qualified literary agent than it is to get a publishing contract. And even if you do get an agent, you still don't have a book deal.

Many unpublished writers have been confronted at one time or another with Publishing's Catch-22, which states: "You can't get a book published without an agent, and you can't get an agent unless you have published a book."

The good news is that the first half is not true (thus rendering it no longer a Catch-22). Many books sold to publishers are, in fact, *unagented* or at least were unagented when submitted.

However, it is true that literary agents are reluctant to take on unpublished clients, and for a very good reason. Agents work solely on commission (10 to 15 percent) and their only "commodities" are time and judgment. Even if a literary agent were to make two or three new finds a year, it is often not worth the time he or she would have to spend in separating the wheat from the chaff. Since literary agents are unsalaried, it is even harder to make your submission part of their business than it is to make it part of an editor's business.

But don't you need a literary agent in order to be taken seriously? This brings up another of those myths that some writers are fond of using to deceive themselves, which is that agents have the credibility and the contacts that the writer lacks ("it is not what you know but who you know").

Agents do have contacts, and this does help them proceed efficiently, as they know the appropriate editor for a work without having to go through the *LMP.* But this is where the usefulness of these contacts ends.

As has been suggested here over and over again, you cannot bluff your way into print. And a literary agent (even if the editor is his or her best friend) cannot bluff on your behalf with any more success than you might have.

The one circumstance under which you probably can get an agent is the one time when you probably think you need one the least, and that is once you have sold your work on your own and it is time to negotiate the contract.

Publishers actually prefer dealing with agents because 1) it separates the deal from the book (it is difficult for a writer to negotiate his or her own contract and then switch roles from businessman back to author), and 2) they "talk the same talk." Both the editor and the agent know what terms of the contract are negotiable and what terms are worth negotiating.

In fact, one way to know a house is dead serious about acquiring your work is when the editor asks you if you do indeed have an agent. If you don't, the editor will probably want to recommend one.

There are situations where an editor may have legitimate reasons for not wanting to recommend an agent, in which case you should refer to the "Literary Agents" listing in the *LMP.* In most cases, however, if the editor expresses some reluctance, this probably means that the house is not as serious about acquiring your work as you had thought.

The good news is that publishing's Catch-22 is not a Catch-22 at all. It is, however, a prudent warning: you don't need a literary agent in order to get published, but once you have taken matters *on your own* to the contract negotiating stage, you are well advised to have one.

THE REJECTION GAME

An editor will never write "We are rejecting your proposal because your idea is bad and your presentation is worse." There are, however, certain phrases publishers use to get off the hook and reject your manuscript as painlessly as possible. But no matter how politely these rejections are worded they are final, so don't read anything encouraging into them.

Some of the most commonly used, politely worded phrases are:

- "We're oversubscribed at this time."
- "We've just acquired a similar title."
- "Your _____ is not right for our list."

If an editor is vaguely interested in your book, there will be nothing circumspect in the response. If he or she doesn't want it, that's it. Move on to the next publisher.

THE PUBLISHING CONTRACT

It seems appropriate to end this chapter with some mention of the publishing contract, since your goal, after all, is to obtain one.

While there are several how-to-get-published books that cover contract negotiation in detail and even delve into promotion and publicity concerns, I have chosen to downplay these topics for two reasons. First, the standard terms of a publishing contract do not vary that much from book to book or from house to house. Other than the number of zeros in the advance (the guaranteed up-front dollars) the deal they will offer to Norman Mailer isn't going to differ that dramatically from what they will offer you.

Second (short of an extraordinary idea or your access to an exceptional property), you are an unproven commodity and you will almost certainly be negotiating from a position of weakness. Track records mean a lot in publishing, and with one successful book under your belt, the negotiating positions will become more equitable. Until then, however, your one paramount, overriding concern about publishing contracts should be in getting one offered to you.

Additionally, where unagented first-time authors are concerned, publishers will often bend over backwards in an effort to be fair. Of publishing's many sins, taking advantage of an author's contract ignorance has never been one of them, and editors will practically assume the role of impartial arbitrator in seeking to reach a mutually beneficial arrangement.

Still, some discussion about what to expect is helpful.

For the average book, of the thirty-odd clauses in a publisher's boilerplate agreement, only about five to ten come into meaningful play. The usual advance for a first-time author is $5,000 to $10,000, though this is an *average* not a standard (there is no such thing as a "standard" advance). Half of the advance is usually received on signing the contract, and the other half when the manuscript is accepted by the publisher. This advance is applied against standard royalties which run 10 percent graduating to 15 percent (of retail price) on hardcovers, 6 to 8 percent on trade paperbacks, and 8 percent on mass market paperbacks.

The publishers will probably ask you for world rights (as opposed to U.S. and Canadian rights), and, lacking a position of strength, you will probably have to agree. Even so, the publisher will probably *volunteer* to give you 75 percent of the income from the sale of foreign rights. (If you don't have an agent, granting a percentage of these rights to the publisher—which has the network in place to sell them—ultimately works to your advantage anyway.)

To suggest, as I have here, that your contract interests are best served by leaving them up to the publisher must certainly sound naive, like recommending a fox to guard your chicken house. But this suggestion fits into a larger context which, before this book can end, must be addressed.

When contemplating book publishing's many awful truths, you must keep in mind one of its bright spots: the people within the industry are, by and large, *not* awful.

Publishing people, on the whole, are of above-average intelligence (some, admittedly, are overeducated) and more well meaning than most. That stubborn, defensive "guard dog mentality" is less prevalent in book publishing than in other businesses, and this bodes well for the would-be author: if you understand the system and your idea has merit, you stand a good shot at getting a fair and reasonable response.

Publishers are also, with rare exception, basically honorable. For some reason, many would-be authors think publishers are going to steal their ideas or "rip them off." As a legal matter, a book idea, per se, cannot be protected by copyright. As a practical matter, an unexecuted or misexecuted book idea is worthless.

The industry is also small. Word of misdeeds or questionable practices travels quickly, and this too contributes to keeping the industry well intentioned and honorable.

Whatever the reasons, publishing has a much more tightly bound unwritten moral and ethical code than most businesses. How many businesses are there, for instance, where an oral commitment (to publish) is as good as a forty-page contract? If an editor says, "I'll buy your book for $10,000," you can start spending, because that statement is as good as cash.

Earlier, I alluded to the glamour and mystique of book publishing, then went on to point out that both were exaggerated. But you are right to want to be a published author. Though it may not always be a profitable experience it is usually a tremendously satisfying one.

And if you can convince an editor to consider, and eventually publish, your work, you are going to find that the people with whom you will be dealing are, in the main, hardworking, smart, and supportive.

ABOUT THE AUTHOR

John Boswell is president of John Boswell Associates, a New York–based literary agency and book-packaging firm, which has packaged or represented over 200 published books.

He is also the author or co-author of five books: *Duke: The John Wayne Album* (Random House); *The U.S. Armed Forces Survival Manual* (Times Books); *The First Family Paperdoll and Cutout Book* (Dell); *Blueprints: 26 Extraordinary Structures* (Simon and Schuster); and most recently the bestselling *What They Don't Teach You at Harvard Business School* (Bantam), which he packaged, agented, and co-wrote with the sports promoter Mark McCormack.

Mr. Boswell began his publishing career as an editor for one of New York's leading publishing houses. As a result, he has been able to observe the publisher's acquisition process from both sides of the editor's desk. It is this dual perspective that he brings to this book.

APPENDIX

Book Proposal for
THE AWFUL TRUTH ABOUT BOOK PUBLISHING*

The idea for this book originally grew out of a luncheon meeting with its editor. Therefore, my formal submission was drawn up to satisfy the essential requirements of a book proposal (as suggested in Chapter Nine), but also to serve as a follow-up to our meeting. I chose, therefore, to present the following proposal in letter form and to define the book's audience in a more general manner than I would have ordinarily. Otherwise, it is a good example of what a book proposal should say and how that information might be organized.

*This was the working title for the book.

143

Ms. Nansey Neiman
Vice-President & Publisher
Warner Books, Inc.
666 Fifth Avenue
New York, NY 10103

Dear Nansey,

As usual it was good seeing you for lunch last week. Your spring list sounds terrific. I'd love to see a catalogue as soon as it is available.

Based on your intuitive understanding of my proposed publishing mini-opus, I've decided to move it up a couple of notches on my priority list. Therefore, please consider the remainder of this letter my proposal for THE AWFUL TRUTH ABOUT BOOK PUBLISHING, subtitled, Why They Always Reject Your Manuscript.

RATIONALE

This is the part you intuitively understand so I'll be brief:

1) There's approximately a 1:1 ratio between people who go into bookstores (i.e. book buyers) and people who have written, are writing, or plan to write a book. Usually they've completed their title and dedication page and want to know what to do next.

2) Since "Do you have any books on how to go about writing a book?" is a frequently asked question of bookstore clerks, this is more counter-displayable than most.

3) Writing and publishing a book remains one of the Great American Dreams, partially because of the prestige of being an "author," but mostly, I think, because the general public still believes that writers make a lot of money. This is one of the myths I'll talk about in Chapter Four, but for now this remains a valid marketing point.

NOT THE RATIONALE

This is not a book of inside publishing gossip or how to
be happily published. It will not tell you how to negotiate
a contract, arrange a publicity tour, or "check up" on your
publisher, since most of the people who buy this book won't
take it that far.

GENERAL PURPOSE

What this book will ultimately show the reader is how to
focus a book, how to get a fair airing for it and how to
get it in front of someone who can make a publishing
decision. It will do this by acknowledging some of the
vinegar-coated realities of the business and presenting
a proposal and submission strategy that meets these
realities head on.

DESCRIPTION

During the five years we have been in business we have
received over four thousand unsolicited inquiries in one
form or another. Since we create most of our books
internally, there are only two that we have taken on and
turned into books. However, since many of these inquiries
are referrals from publishers, clients, friends, or simply
people to whom I've made the mistake of revealing what
I do, some response is often required.

As a result I have developed a litany of aphorisms, quotes,
anecdotes, statistics, and one-liners that allows me to turn
down a project as quickly, as painlessly, and as absolutely
as possible. Even those absolute statements that are only
90 percent true "sound right" -- they contain a kernel of
publishing truth which even a publishing outsider can
understand.

It occurred to me that not only is this information
desirable to a large segment of the book-buying public, it
can also be organized into obvious chapters of facts, good
news, bad news, how publishing really works, etc.

which, as you will see, roughly forms the first half of the outline for the book I'm proposing.

Finally, I believe that I can spend an hour with almost anyone and, by asking the right questions, shape a book for them that can actually be published, albeit probably not very profitably. I have actually done this (or had to do it) on several occasions. In the second half of the book I will run through this process, then show the reader how to focus a book, write a proposal, and get it in front of someone who might be interested in publishing it. I will also throw in some do's and don'ts and some questions to ask oneself before spending several years writing an autobiographical novel or another cookbook.

STYLE, TONE, AND THE ANSWER TO AN OBVIOUS QUESTION

Why would anyone want to buy such a negative little bubble-bursting book? Because it's actually a positive little bubble-making book. If I do my job correctly, the facts that I present up front will only serve to support the soundness of the advice offered later on. (To underscore this point I suggest the use of a cover line "Publishing Realities -- And How to Take Advantage of Them" or a longer subtitle: Why They Always Reject Your Manuscript -- And What to Do About It.) Moreover, any book that suggests that book publishing can sometimes be vague and inefficient can only warm the hearts of oft-rejected aspiring authors.

The tone will be direct and a bit dictatorial, and though blows will occasionally be cushioned with humor, I see this in style, tone, and form as an UP THE ORGANIZATION for would-be writers. Though Townsend's book was written in 1970 I believe it is the prototype for informational books of the 1980's: short chunks of text under multi-subheadings; irreverent and iconoclastic in tone; and in a form that can be quickly absorbed by bottom line thinkers.

I also hope the book will contain a bit of unconventional wisdom, as most of what I have to say flies directly in the face of the pablum spooned out by writers' conferences and writers' magazines, and the advice I've seen offered in other books on the subject (misleading aspiring writers is a big business).

CHAPTER OUTLINE FOR
THE AWFUL TRUTH ABOUT BOOK PUBLISHING

(Note 1: Some of the figures I use are old and will of course be updated and reverified for the book. Note 2: Though I've got an example to illustrate each point I make, I'll try to confine myself here to one or two per chapter.)

INTRODUCTION

Wherein I will establish my credentials for writing this book, challenge its readers ("What makes you think you can write a book?"), then tell them how this book is going to help them.

An editor friend once told me of being chastised by an agent for rejecting an unpublishable novel which should never have been submitted in the first place:

> "You know what they say," the agent said, "everyone has at least one book in them."

> "That may be true," my friend said, "but I don't have to publish it."

The lesson of that exchange and of the introduction will be that yes, you probably do have a book in you, but you better figure out if it's the one someone might want to publish.

CHAPTER ONE: PUBLISH AND BE DAMNED:
A BRIEF TRUE HISTORY
OF BOOK PUBLISHING IN AMERICA

Wherein I will explain, in five pages or less, how a hobby

for men of independent means attempted to become a business.

CHAPTER TWO: THE DEPRESSING FACTS

Wherein I will explain some of the verifiable realities of book publishing that are germane to the would-be author. For example:

-- There were 50,000 new books published last year. Suppose the soup industry decided that within the next twelve months it was going to introduce 50,000 new brands of soup into your supermarket. Tomato (THE JOY OF SEX) and Cream of Mushroom (THE HOLY BIBLE) would continue to do well, but Campbell's "Cream of Chunky Lentil (your book)" would most likely fall between the cracks.

-- Books are not food, shelter, or clothing.

-- Only 35 percent of Americans have read a book since high school.

-- Only 20 percent of Americans have ever been in a bookstore.

-- Books are sold on consignment. That means you have to sell it twice (the author, of course, three times), once to the bookstore owner and once to the guy who carries it out the front door. (All the hardships created by returns -- including that in hard times books become negotiable currency between publisher and seller -- will be discussed.)

CHAPTER THREE: HOW IT WORKS
AND WHY IT OFTEN DOESN'T

Wherein I will explain the basic structure of a publishing house, lists, patterns, formats, distribution channels, sales conferences ("The Lemmings Go to Puerto Rico"), etc.

CHAPTER FOUR: WHAT IT ALL MEANS TO YOU

What happens once you've licked the stamp, closed the envelope and placed your proposal, manuscript, etc., c/o Acme House, in the hands of the U.S. Postal Service? Slush pile explained. Editor's workday explained (overworked, underpaid, acquiring one book for next spring, working on another for this fall, correcting galleys for next month, and finding out why B. Dalton never received their order today); publishers' schizophrenia explained (attracted to publishing because they love books only to discover that's a distraction).

I'd like to include some sample reader's reports and some sample rejection letters with humorous but instructive call-outs. (Example: Rejection letter salutation -- "Dear Sir or Madam" or "Dear _____" Call-out: "James Michener doesn't get a letter from his publisher where the 'Dear' and 'Mr. Michener' are typed in different typefaces."

CHAPTER FIVE: MYTHS, MISCONCEPTIONS, AND SAD IRONIES

Examples:

-- Authors make a lot of money. This myth gets perpetuated because when Judith Krantz sells the paperback rights to her novel for 3.2 million dollars it's reported on the front page of The New York Times. When Judith Schwartz sells the paperback rights to her novel for high two figures not even her best friend knows. I'll quote the Columbia University report, etc.

-- The Publishing Catch-22: "You have to have a book published in order to get an agent; you have to have an agent in order to publish a book." Not true. Over half the books sold are unagented. Publishers usually prefer to deal with agents because "they talk the same talk." An agent can't get a book published which is not otherwise publishable. Good agents act as winnowers, separating wheat from chaff, which is how they maintain their credibility.

This myth is perpetuated because the Publishing Catch-22 is one of the best ironclad excuses, used by both agents and publishers, for rejecting a manuscript.

-- Just keep trying. The ole "papered my room with rejection slips" myth.

-- Publishing has some relation to literature.

-- Once you've published a book, you're "home free" -- i.e. you can always get another one published. Au contraire, the truth of the "sophomore slump."

CHAPTER SIX: A LITTLE GOOD NEWS

Some Examples:

-- There were over 50,000 new titles published last year. That's a lot of books. If the idea is simply to get a book published, the bane of the publishing business can be seen as a boon to aspiring authors. Your odds of getting a book published are certainly much better than, say, becoming Pope or getting your name in THE GUINNESS BOOK OF WORLD RECORDS.

-- There's this wonderful concept called royalties. That's the nicest thing about a book contract -- you're protected in the event of success. (A discussion of how book royalties work is the closest I'll get to discussing contracts.)

-- Publishers are basically honest. For some reason, many would-be writers think publishers are going to steal their ideas or "rip them off." As a legal matter, a book idea, per se, is not copyrightable. As a practical matter, an unexecuted or misexecuted idea is worthless. Even if publishers were crooks, there is no motivation.

In general, publishing has a much more tightly bound unwritten moral and ethical code than most businesses. In what other business is a verbal contract agreement almost as good as cash?

-- Publishing people, on the whole, are of above average intelligence and more well meaning than most. That German shepherd security guard mentality is less prevalent in book publishing than in other businesses. This bodes well for the would-be author: if you understand the system, and if the book has some publishing merit, the chances are it will receive a considered response.

-- Yes, I can. Several first-time-out bestsellers and slush pile success stories.

<u>CHAPTER SEVEN: IF YOU MUST</u>

(This is the bone with the most meat on it and by far the longest chapter in the book. I'm not adverse to breaking this up into several chapters.)

John D. MacDonald once told me that on those occasions when he rubs elbows with his public the two comments he most often hears are the two that irritate him the most. The first is, "Hey, I've got a great idea for a novel for you." In so many words he politely explains that the last thing a successful novelist needs is someone else's idea.

The second comment is, "Hey, I'm writing a book too!" "Look," MacDonald said to me, "I'm a professional writer. This is what I do for a living, but for some reason, everyone thinks they should be able to do what I do.

"Can you imagine someone going up to Horowitz and saying, 'I've been thinking about giving a recital at Carnegie Hall myself.' Or to Wyeth: 'I do a little painting now and then, who should I approach for a one-man show, the National Gallery or the Met?'

"I guess it has to do with the fact that people write letters or postcards or laundry lists, so why not a book?

"It's a little bit harder than that."

The first part of this chapter will be "What Makes You Think You Can Write a Book and Other Questions You Should Ask Yourself" wherein I will force the reader to carefully examine his or her motivations. Some examples, all of which will be fully explained in the text:

-- Do you want to be "an author" or do you want to write?

-- Is there anything in your experience or background that indicates you have a talent for writing?

-- Is there anything in your experience or background that someone would pay $15 to read about?

-- Are you a "sprinter" or a "marathoner"?

-- Do you finish what you start, even when the light at the end of the tunnel looks like Betelgeuse? What other tasks have you completed where you knew, before you began, it would be a six- to twelve-month effort?

From here I will offer one- and two-paragraph summaries of the most prevalent publishing categories and some of the realities affecting each. Some examples:

FICTION -- You probably can't write fiction because almost no one can. Though commercial fiction may not be art, it is certainly a very special craft mastered by few. Many frustrated writers rationalize that their fiction is too "literary" -- i.e. too good -- for the marketplace. That's an excuse for not being able to tell a good story.

There is almost no way to judge if you are some latent fiction talent who simply hasn't been discovered yet, though good fiction writing does not seem to require super intelligence or a particular background. Colleen McCullough, before she wrote THORNBIRDS, was a nurse, Rosemary Rogers, a secretary, Judith Krantz, an ad agency exec, and Judith Guest, a housewife.

It does seem to have something to do with the ability "to run a movie inside your head" -- an intuitive story sense that plays out scene by scene. An understanding of human nature (characterization, motivation, etc.) also helps.

Not surprising, a number of actors (a profession that combines intuition and training) have made the successful transition to bestselling novelists, including Tom Tryon, Robert Ludlum, and Jackie Susann.

COOKBOOKS -- More cookbooks are published annually than any other type of book. Yet this is a "brand name" business dominated by the Julia Childs and James Beards and "Betty Crockers" of the world, and the magazines that service the woman's market (Family Circle, Woman's Day, etc.). One woman, desperate to get her cookbook published, told me she was even willing to change her last name to "BetterHomesandGardens."

Your best bet -- in a market that really doesn't have any best bets -- is to concentrate on regional or specialty cooking that may not, as yet, have had its day of fame. Many of the successful specialty cookbooks have been geared to whatever the hot, new specialty appliance happens to be. Here, it's usually the firstest with the mostest. Several years ago a woman by the name of Mabel Hoffman wrote a cookbook entitled CROCKERY COOKERY. It sold over a million copies. Recent "hot" appliances have been the food processor and the microwave oven.

CHILDREN'S BOOKS -- Many first-time authors attempt children's books because they think it is one of the easier forms of writing. In fact, it is one of the hardest. Normally, the form these never-to-be-published stories take is a simplistic, and often simple-minded, tale that ends with a moral.

Children <u>hate</u> blatant moralizing. They love books because they allow them to escape into a world of fantasy, and a moral at the end of a story only serves to jerk them back to a world of reality. Read the bestselling authors in this genre, a Sendak or a Dr. Seuss, and you will see these books are often dominated by naughty, even mean, little characters.

The best children's books are those that appeal not just to children but to the child in everyone.

Part Two of this chapter will be called "So What Should I Write About" and it is designed to help the reader focus his or her market and then focus the prospective book for that market.

FOCUSING A MARKET UP AND THEN DOWN -- The biggest potential market is one that includes every man, woman, and child in the United States, but appealing to everyone is the same as appealing to no one. The best market for a book is one that is significant in terms of its overall number (say, the owners of home computers, which now exceed 20 million) but is <u>specific</u> enough so that a significant percentage of that number will say, "This is a book for me."

To help the reader determine a topic or subject, I will again ask a series of leading questions. Some examples, all of which will be fully explained:

    -- What do you do well? Do you have an expertise? (If not, meet an expert.)

-- What do you do, or what experience have you had, that people seem curious about?

-- Is there any topic on which friends invariably turn to you for advice?

General advice will include: Follow pop trends, pop shows ("60 Minutes") and pop magazines ("People") analyze social movements (i.e. the new baby boom), and read between the lines of bestseller lists.

Once the reader has a topic in mind and understands its potential market, it is time to ask the two most significant make-or-break questions:

-- What percentage of my potential market <u>goes into bookstores</u>? Here I will use the example of auto racing, which combined (trans am, stocks, Formula I, drag, etc.) is the number one spectator sport in the United States (60 million annually). Yet only seven of them have ever been in a bookstore!

-- What else has been done on the subject (i.e. know your competition)? Here I will introduce THE SUBJECT GUIDE TO BOOKS IN PRINT, available at any library and as a reference at many bookstores. Amazingly, all the books that purport to give would-be writers advice rarely emphasize the importance of this particular volume. Harking back to Chapter Two, I will advise that if there are fifteen to twenty titles listed under a particular subject, that in itself is not cause for alarm. If there are two hundred that's at least cause for pause.

Now that the reader has been somewhat sobered by what he or she has discovered I will offer some suggestions and examples on how to make an idea special. Books are set in cold type and it is important to humanize your subject, to identify with your reader. One way is to ask yourself the question "What does my potential reader feel (as opposed to think)?" For instance, using an earlier example, if the idea is a Beginner Guide to Home Computers, you might say to yourself that computers being computers, there is probably some feeling of intimidation on the part of a novice or prospective home computer owner. Don't be afraid to acknowledge that. Such a book might be called "A Plain Language Guide to Home Computers" or "Home Computers For Math Dropouts."

Some of the other suggestions for shaping an idea:

-- Get a "fix" on your reader (write out a "psycho profile").
-- Understand the subliminal motivation a reader may have to buying your book. Example: THIN THIGHS IN THIRTY DAYS equals "I'll look beautiful in a month."
-- Say what you mean. Pretend you're having a conversation with your reader.
-- Get your idea accredited.
-- Add a fake "brand name."

Finally, I will ask the readers to analyze their potential book project in terms of "doability." It may be that their conclusion is to ghost Frank Sinatra's autobiography or to rewrite the Encyclopedia Britannica. In both cases the "doability quotient" is extremely low.

Part Three of this chapter will focus on "The Great American Proposal" or how to fill a few sheets of paper in a way that will separate a publisher from his money.

Jim Bouton, author of the bestselling BALL FOUR, speaks every year to forty or fifty college creative writing classes. His message: Forget about the bon mot, the well-turned phrase, or the beautifully rendered short story; learn to write a good proposal.

Throughout the book I plan to gently discourage the would-be fiction writer. At some point during this chapter I will digress into a short section and explanation of the unique character and requirements of a fiction proposal. However, most of the book, and particularly this chapter, is obviously focused toward non-fiction for the obvious reason that this is an area where an unpublished writer will have his best shot.

There are two overall considerations for a book proposal: (1) A good book proposal; it is less an example of writing style than it is a justification of why the book should be published in the first place. Succinctly tell what the book is about, who's going to buy it and why, how it's organized, and why you're qualified to write it. (2) The outline section of the proposal should sound like the book is already written and that you are merely summarizing it for the convenience of the publisher.

I have a specific non-fiction proposal form that I recommend which has worked very well. I will break this down into its seven components and analyze each. Two examples:

-- The Opening: "First You Have to Get His Attention." What is the best thing you can say about your book that will make someone keep reading (hint: It's not "This is a really good book")? It may be an extracted line or story or anecdote that dramatically illustrates the quality of your material. It may be a simple statement that reveals the size of your potential audience. Two of the best I've seen, which aren't very applicable but certainly illustrate the point are "I'm prepared to spend $100,000 to promote my book entitled _____" and, from ex-astronaut Pete Conrad's proposal: "I did not sleep very well the night before I went to the moon."

-- The Outline: Go back to the sixth grade and begin
with the standard outline form -- Roman numeral
I, big "A," little "a," etc. Research until your
outline -- and chapters -- are balanced. Convert to
short narrative summary, using short sentences
or sentence fragments. Use colons, semicolons,
dashes, and parentheses to separate big "A" from
little "a." Give one or two examples in each chapter,
preferably ones that sound like "I've got a million
of 'em, but to save time, here's a couple."

I also plan to include one or two good sample proposals,
give some good advice (Ex: Conjure up good company by
suggesting bestsellers that you feel are similar in style,
form, or content to your book) and answer obvious
questions (Ex: Q: How long should a proposal be? A: As
long as it has to be to say everything you want to say
-- and no longer).

The fourth and final section of this chapter will concentrate
on "Submission Strategy," which will include a discussion
of when and why a publisher is most likely to be "open
for business," how to use the LMP effectively (to determine
a house's "personality" as well as who to contact), and
the proper structure of a submission letter that will demand
a response.

This section will begin with a disclaimer, perhaps even
a "money back guarantee" -- "that if you skip to this chapter
without reading and absorbing that which has preceded
it, I can guarantee that your book will never be published."

It will also include a discussion about titles. Though the
title of any unsolicited proposal is likely to change, a good
title, which says everything in a few words, can get the
attention of an editor faster than anything else. This

discussion will also illustrate the kinds of titles to avoid
-- pun-traps, pregnant-with-irony, cutesy, oxymoronic, non
sequiturs, etc.

Throughout this final (overly long) chapter I will
intersperse several "Do's and Don'ts," "Q and A's," and
similar features which perhaps graphically could be
treated as sidebar material. For instance, vis-a-vis the
solicitation letter section I plan to include a list of "Dead
Giveaways" ("This is a humorous book about..."; "My friends
have read it and they all love it"; "Perhaps my style is
too literary, but..."; a design for cover art; "This is your
next bestseller"; etc.).

ILLUSTRATIONS

Illustrations are not essential to the text but I do think
they could prove very helpful in graphically opening up
the book, and demystifying its contents, and in general
making this material more accessible to the reader.

I would propose a limited use of graphs, charts, and the
aforementioned call-outs, particularly when these graphic
devices would prove more informative than text. For
instance, in distinguishing between a front list and back
list book while also emphasizing the sheer difficulty of
selling any book I could envision the following graphic
representation:

FRONT   BACK   NORMAL

I would also like to include some illustrations by a professional illustrator/friend of mine. Some samples of his work are enclosed.

Finally, as predictable as this may sound I'm going to bring it up anyway. Over the years some wonderful publishing cartoons have appeared in <u>The New Yorker</u>. Three come immediately to mind:

-- Him to Her at a Hamilton-drawn cocktail party: "No, none of my work has been published, but I have had two manuscripts professionally typed."

-- Editor to Author who is sitting next to Ernest Hemingway lookalike: "Mr. Forbish this is Blake Dawson. We'll be using his photo on your dust jacket."

-- Uncaptioned cartoon of bookstore interior with "fiction," "biography," and "non-book" sections clearly labeled, the latter including volumes with faucets, propeller beanies, and other absurd paraphernalia protruding between the covers.

SPECIFICATIONS

I envision this book to be a 6" x 9" trade paperback, preferably horizontally bound, of 128 to 160 pages in length. The text will run approximately 30,000 words.

I am willing to deliver text/illustrations, mechanicals, or bound books.

In conclusion, Nansey, I have obviously run on longer than intended with this little epistle, which I hope you will see is some measure of the passion I have for this project.

I honestly feel it is a book that will help those millions of aspiring writers out there, if for no other reason than it does not mislead them. If the result is not more books worthy of publication, I hope it will at least improve the quality of everyone's slush pile. On second thought, maybe I should write this under a pseudonym -- and you should publish it as "Acme House."

We look forward to your response.

Yours sincerely,

John Boswell
President

JB:pb
enclosures